Scott

MY SIDETRACKS
AS AN ENTREPRENEUR

Best of Business!

Gary   2/18/25

MY SIDETRACKS
AS AN ENTREPRENEUR

True Stories and Life Lessons
for Successful Business Leadership

GARY OBERG, BME, PE

Rose City Press,
Litchfield, Minnesota

Rose City Press
PO Box L
Dassel, Minnesota 55325

Website: www.mysidetracks.com

ISBN 9798579467775

BISAC CODES
BIO003000   BIOGRAPHY & AUTOBIOGRAPHY / Business
BUS025000   BUSINESS & ECONOMICS / Entrepreneurship
TEC019000   TECHNOLOGY & ENGINEERING / Lasers & Photonics

Book Cover Design Art Director: Joan Holman

To Ginny, Dawn, and Troy

CONTENTS

"I'm not going to tell the story the way it happened. I'm going to tell it the way I remember it."

—CHARLES DICKENS,
Great Expectations

PREFACE

SHARING MY PROFESSIONAL EXPERIENCE SEEMS a bit scary. I am an introvert and I like privacy. In elementary school and high school, I was scared silly to talk in front of a group. Even through college I did everything I could to not have to stand up in front of a class and give a presentation.

I did not overcome this fear of speaking in front of a crowd until I attended a Dale Carnegie course in Rochester, Minnesota. I came out of my shell and learned how to control my emotions and fear, and yes, I beat the table with a rolled up newspaper!

Even though there is no one here in this room with me, I still feel that old tremor when I think about sharing my career story and advice. However, over the years, I have learned to avoid fears. Nearly all fears never come to fruition,

I feel blessed to have grown up on a farm and followed the American dream. I lived through the sweet spot of technology like the jet engine, transistor, internet, laser technology, and of course many other innovations. I lived to see my father farm with horses and to watch my contemporary farm friends farm with GPS-controlled tractors and combines. I have seen medical advancements that controlled polio, to the latest bio-absorbable stents to treat heart disease. I have lived through the Korean Conflict (where my uncle Eldridge served), the Cold War, the Vietnam War, Gulf War, Afghanistan War, and the Iraq War.

I was a prime age for the Vietnam War. I looked at my options and decided this was not a good one to volunteer for. I decided to live my life such that if I were drafted, I would serve. Fortunately, I did not get drafted.

I have learned to be brutally honest about my strengths and weaknesses. My weakness was sales and marketing. I do not enjoy marketing myself. However, I did find that I was pretty good at sales in a job-shop setting. This is better classified as consultative sales. It involves solving a customer's problem around your processing capability. I really enjoyed this aspect of business.

I have spent a lot of time on leading-edge laser processing applications. I have achieved some degree of success but that is not a singular achievement. I needed good colleagues and employees around me, and of course a loving and supportive wife and family. I do not know anyone who has made it in a vacuum.

I hope that I can paint a picture of what an entrepreneur has to go through to be successful and to avoid my mistakes and pitfalls. You may benefit of my experience in a job shop that transitioned to a product company. You will learn what not to do in China. You will learn how to deal with a bully.

This book is not about the history of any one company, but several, each playing a role in my career development.

Enjoy my sidetracks, learn some things, and hopefully be amused.

FOREWORD

"If you would not be forgotten,
As soon as you are dead and rotten,
Either write things worth reading,
Or do things worth writing."
                    —BENJAMIN FRANKLIN

Lives of great men all remind us
    We can make our lives sublime,
And, departing, leave behind us
    Footprints on the sands of time;

Footprints, that perhaps another,
    Sailing o'er life's solemn main,
A forlorn and shipwrecked brother,
    Seeing, shall take heart again.
                    —HENRY WADSWORTH
                        LONGFELLOW

WHEN I SAID TO GARY OBERG, "You ought to write another book," he replied that he wasn't so sure he should do so.

He had already put a great deal of time and work into writing his first book, *Sidetracks: 40 True Stories of Hunting and Fishing on Paths Less Traveled,* and was enjoying much positive feedback and success with that book. So maybe he should just settle for the one book.

But I still thought Gary had another important book to

write, one that could be interesting and also helpful for other people. A book that dealt with the entrepreneurial and business side of his life.

So, I said to him:

> "*Sidetracks* is a personal book with true stories about your hunting and fishing adventures, and it's great. But I think you should write a book related to your success in business as an entrepreneur. You are a very good storyteller and I know you have some stories about that part of your life as well. And I believe you should share something about your business experiences and leave that wisdom as part of your legacy.
>
> To tell you the truth, when I agreed to help you with marketing for your original *Sidetracks* book, I wasn't really sure about its potential. Very few books sell many copies and there are millions of books out there as well as almost unlimited digital media that are competing for people's attention.
>
> Although I thought your book was very well written, I just wasn't sure about its potential in a crowded and uncertain marketplace. These days with so many people writing books, it's hard to even get someone to read a free review copy, let alone purchase an actual copy of a book.
>
> When your book turned out to be so successful, I knew that people liked your storytelling and your writing, so I feel encouraged that there will also be interest in other books you write. And, if your book about your experiences as an entrepreneur can help others on their own path to success, I think it would be worth it to make the effort to do another book."

An important part of my life's mission has been to showcase and preserve the true stories of great achievers, of individuals from all walks of life and all kinds of backgrounds who have overcome adversity to leave a positive legacy.

For most of my lifetime I have been studying successful individuals and the principles that underpin all great achievement.

My interest in the *Science of Success* led me to create and produce the *Legacy of Achievement* television program, which featured many high achievers from all walks of life, and which was broadcast on PBS television stations nationally.

My program presented for the first time on public television the teachings from the bestselling book *Think and Grow Rich* by Napoleon Hill.

It was hosted by Dr. Dennis Kimbro, co-author with Napoleon Hill of *Think and Grow Rich: A Black Choice.*

As the most read self-help book of all time, *Think and Grow Rich* was first published in 1937, and went on to sell over 100 million copies. Called the granddaddy of all motivational literature, the book is based upon 20 years of Hill's research of some of the most successful individuals of his generation.

Gary Oberg's success exemplifies the principles of achievement found in the *Think and Grow Rich* philosophy. And much can be learned from his success in business.

Over 25 years ago, I established the Legacy of Achievement Foundation, which was dedicated to preserving the lives and lessons of great achievers through the creation of an original media archive featuring contemporary high achievers.

Not the rich and famous, but people I called the "jewels." People who were not only successful but who also exemplified such positive characteristics as integrity, compassion, honor, faith, courage, kindness, and goodness.

I am very pleased that Gary Oberg finally agreed to write his second book and preserve some of his own legacy of achievement through the publication of *My Sidetracks as An Entrepreneur* because I believe we can learn a lot about success and achievement by studying the lives of those who have been successful. And he has been very successful!

We can also learn a lot by being in the presence of successful individuals, and reading a book written in their own words creates a very special connection with them.

In life, if we are fortunate, we can have a successful mentor. The guidance, help, and example by someone who has achieved what we are also hoping to achieve can be invaluable.

If we are not able to have a living mentor or example in our lives, we can still seek out connections with those individuals whom we know have the attainment we wish to also have, with those individuals who have achieved what we wish to achieve. With those individuals who have qualities we wish to cultivate.

We can do this by accessing their writings, interviews with them and so on.

The Indian philosophy concept of "darshan" states that the holding of an image of a revered person results in the human viewer's receiving a blessing from that person. When applied to the *Science of Success*, this can mean that just being in the presence of someone, living or dead, through a visual or written, or other means of connection, can transmit positive energy from that person to us personally.

Those who go before us leave their "footprints in the sands of time."

And we can tap into these footprints through writings, audios, videos, and other means of communications that allow us to be in their presence and learn from them.

And in today's online world, leaving a digital footprint can last forever and reach almost everyone on the planet.

Thank you, Gary, for sharing the gift of your legacy for posterity!

Joan Holman, M.A.

- Author, Producer, Acclaimed Internet Guru

- Author of *Hands That Touch, Hands That Heal,* the biography of renowned massage pioneer Sister Rosalind Gefre (Sister Rosalind Christian Ministries 2003)

- Featured notable woman in the book *Dear Success Seeker: Wisdom from Outstanding Women* by Michele R. Wright, PhD (Simon & Schuster 2009)

- Creator of the PBS Television Program, *The Legacy of Achievement* (Featuring the "Lives and Legacies of Great Achievers"

1 • MY EARLY SIDETRACKS

WHEN I WAS ABOUT TWELVE years old, I saved up $17.00 and bought a brand-new jigsaw from a Sears mail-order catalogue. I scrounged around and found an old washing machine motor to power it and I went into business. I found some from scrap pieces of lumber and plywood and used them to cut out lawn ornaments. I painted them up and sold them to the relatives, which turned out to be an easy sell, but I soon ran out of relatives and my business dried up.

I guess that was my first experience of learning the importance sales and marketing. At the same time, I learned that my skills were not in that area, so, I decided to suck back and regroup. Still, I had a taste of what it was to make my own money; to earn. I had become an entrepreneur.

Next, I started a pocket gopher-trap-line with my horse, Spirit. That was a pretty good business since I lived in the Gopher State of Minnesota. I got twenty-five cents bounty from the Spruce Hill Town Board for each pair of front feet. The farmers hated gophers because of the many mounds they would leave in the field. The piles of dirt could cause damage to the farm equipment. I provided a worthy service.

On a good day, I could catch three or four gophers. Not bad money considering I could buy a candy bar for a nickel or a double dip ice cream cone for a dime. It was easy money, but seasonal. The gophers were stupid and easy to catch early in the spring but as the summer wore on, they got wise to my traps and difficult to catch.

I also made a little money catching striped gophers, although I only got five cents each for the stripers. To catch them I would lay a snare around the mouth of a gopher hole and when they popped their heads up, I'd pull the twine noose around them.

Sometimes I'd use a more barbarous method by taking a wire, sharpening both ends, and then bending it into a U and then turning the ends of the wire inward. I'd attach about a ten-foot string to the bend and then place it over the gopher hole. I'd give a sharp whistle and when the striper came up to see what the noise was, I'd give a quick tug and out it came, impaled at the neck. It might have been a bit more brutal, but I had fewer get away.

I wanted to trap muskrat, but we lived too far from a good rat pond, so I tried trapping weasels and mink instead.

"Gary," my dad said when I told him that I wanted to trap mink, which would fetch me ten bucks each, "why don't you put up a trap in the creek near the house?"

"Oh yeah?" I was interested in what he had in mind. "How would that work?"

"You set your trap in the shallow water, ask your mom to save the chicken heads for you, then put a head on a stick over the top of the trap. When a mink or a weasel comes along and tries to take the chicken head, it'll get stuck in the shallow water."

Well, that seemed like a pretty good way to go, so I tried it. I never did get a mink, but I did get some weasels that were worth about a buck each. Good one Dad!

The next year I decided to try raising cucumbers. This was a backbreaking job and the cucumbers had prickles on them that were nasty on the hands. I picked them early in the morning when the dew was still on the leaves and that made it all the nastier. The cannery needed the cucumbers early in the day. The pickle factory lasted but I didn't.

The town of Hewitt, where the pickle factory was located, launched an annual pickle festival. I remember you could buy a hat that had a stuffed pickle sticking out of it. They always had a big parade with all kinds of bizarre floats. They had a bed race with a pretty girl laying on the bed and four young bucks pushing the bed, which was on rollers; that was a little different.

Another feature was an antique tractor pull. The Pickle Days are still going to this day. It makes me smile to think that some things never change.

From raising the nasty cucumbers, I graduated to growing navy beans. These were edible beans that I raised in my mother's garden. My mom took it upon herself to teach me how to plant, care for, and harvest the beans. This was much easier work and they were simple to plant and raise. I didn't have to do much of anything till they turned brown in the fall. Once brown, I pulled them out by the roots and thrashed them in a fifty-five-gallon barrel. The beans would drop to the bottom of the barrel. Then I would winnow them on a blanket on a breezy day. I packaged them in one-pound bags and sold them to the same relatives who bought my lawn ornaments, but this time I had more success in selling to neighbors too.

My first hourly job was building hog pens for my uncle Dewayne. We used rough-sawed oak lumber that was about as hard as cement. That was where I really learned how to pound a nail.

"Gary," said my uncle, "whatcha gotta do is rub the nail into your hair a little. That way, the nail gets greased a bit and goes in easier."

I looked at him sideways and asked, "Are you pulling my leg?"

"Not at all! Not at all!" to which he picked up a nail, rubbed it against his sunburned scalp, and then effortlessly hammered it home.

I gave it a try, but I guess my shampoo must have been better than his because half the nails I used ended up being bent. My uncle paid me ten cents an hour, but if he'd have been smart, he would have paid me by the number of straight nails I hammered home. I kept that opinion to myself.

My first off-the-farm job was laying sod for a housing contractor near Alexandria, Minnesota. This paid a dollar per hour, which was big money for me. After work I would stop in the drug store in Alexandria to visit my girlfriend, Ginny, who was a soda jerk at Peterson Drug.

Ginny was the prettiest girl I'd ever seen. Besides her good looks, she was able to see past my dirty clothes, unlike the druggist, all dressed in a clean white uniform. I'd come into the store covered in black dirt dust and he'd give me a look even dirtier than my clothes. That never bothered me though. Nothing bothered me when I went to see my lovely girlfriend.

I would slurp down a soda and slip out the back door. As I walked away, I looked back and thought that I wouldn't always just be the contractor's sod-layer, that someday I wanted to be the contractor. There's maybe nothing so motivating as the love of a good woman.

* * * *

2 • ONE THING LEADS TO ANOTHER IN MINNESOTA

FATHER LOUIS HENNEPIN, A BELGIAN Roman Catholic priest, set out in the late 1600s on a mission to evangelize the Indians along the Mississippi River, in the area that is now Minneapolis and Saint Paul, Minnesota.

As Father Hennepin spread the word of God, he also brought back word of the vast and mature forests that graced the lands he'd visited. He could not have imagined what the great land he'd discovered would someday become.

Loggers listened closely to his descriptions of endless forests. They soon followed the priest's footsteps and found more timber than they could imagine. Any trees that weren't suitable for lumber were claimed by the newly blooming paper industry. More industrious folks thought, "OK, we have all this paper, we might as well do some printing right here in Minnesota."

Thus, the graphic arts industry was launched.

The graphic arts industry, through its printing technology, eventually lead to the printed circuit business. This was a foundation for the supercomputing companies: Remington Rand, Control Data, and Cray Research.

Meanwhile, in the early 1800s, two brothers were born in small-town Minnesota: William and Charles Mayo. These babies grew up to be two very remarkable physicians, specialists in surgery, and medical pioneers. With the help of the Franciscan

Sisters and their St. Mary's Hospital, the Mayo brothers built up an operative clinic that would become the now world-renown Mayo Clinic.

Among many advancements and inventions, the marriage between the printed circuit industry and the medical technology movement, came the development of the pacemaker by Medtronic. This particular invention launched a whole new medical development phase, which continues to this day. For my part, I started a company called Spectralytics, which uses laser technology to make medical devices.

So, you could say that my own career all started with a mission and a big beautiful Minnesota pine tree.

● ● ● ●

3 • A FARMING TEST

WHEN YOU THINK OF ENTREPRENEURSHIP, farming probably is one of the last occupations that comes to mind. In fact, farmers are a special lot of people, and in many ways, they are the ultimate entrepreneurs.

I grew up on a Minnesota dairy farm and I thought I knew farming. From my home on a dairy farm, I moved to many different places and only moved back to my roots: the Minnesota 7th Congressional District. The 7th District has the most agriculture in the nation and covers almost all of the western side of Minnesota except for the far south. Cities in the district include Alexandria (where I attended high school), Fergus Falls, Willmar and Moorhead.

Since returning to my childhood home area where farming still continues, I've learned that the only similarities to today's modern dairy farm are cows, milk, and cow dung!

Farming was always hard work and involved high risk, but the farming business of today requires not only hard work, but also careful risk assessment, risk management, constant innovation, and the effective use of technology and modern farming methods. Gone are the days of milking Bessy by hand. Today robotic milking is the newest technology. If today's farmer is to be competitive, to stay with the times. As much as I understood farming from my dad's generation, I've learned from my modern-day Minnesota farming friends that there is so much more to it now.

My wife, Ginny (yes, the cute soda jerk from the drug store), and I spend a few winter months at our home in Tucson, Arizona, but most of our year is spent at our home in rural Minnesota, where I attend a men's Bible study on Tuesday mornings at 6:00 AM. It's one of my weekly highlights to share fellowship with a dozen farmers in the group. While I do enjoy all of their company, I prefer hanging out with guys who shower after work.

These farmers have a lot of faith in family and God. Most of them never turn a wheel on the Sabbath. This takes a lot of fortitude when the harvest is ripe and the weather is good. The entrepreneurial stakes are high. I often wonder what I would do in that situation, but I'll probably will never know because I will not be put to that test.

That is not to say I haven't been tested in other farming ways.

This past year I did some pro bono work for Blake, one of my farm buddies. In return, he coached me in some of the modern farming techniques.

"Okay Gary," said Blake, "I'm going to put you on that tractor over there and you're going to go alongside the combine so he can fill the tractor with corn. Then you're going to take the corn over to that semi-trailer over there and transfer the load."

Blake was a blonde man with a medium build and medium height, who took his farming—and most things—very seriously.

"Alright," I said, "sounds simple enough."

Blake kind of looked at me through squinted blue eyes, crinkled from seasons of working in the sun and said, "Yeaaaaah . . . it might be simple but it's not quite as easy as you might think."

"How hard can it be?" I asked, naively.

Blake threw his head back and laughed hard—belly-laugh hard. He was a serious man having a good laugh: that's when I had my first inkling that this might not be the cakewalk I thought it would be.

"Tell you what," Blake said, "you'll sit in the driver's seat and I'll position myself beside you so's I can keep an eye on things and let you know what to do."

I still thought this might be a bit of overkill, but okay, who am I to tell him what to do with his business?

"Sounds good," I said.

As we walked the distance to the tractor, Blake explained that they use a computer program to lay out a GPS track for both the tractor and planter to follow. Earlier in the year, the planter injected a kernel of corn into the ground at precisely six inches apart. The same program was used for the spraying operation, and now the harvest combine operation that we were about to embark upon.

I climbed up into the plush driver's seat and enjoyed the feel and comfort of the machine. For a guy who's worked either in an office, a boat, or a factory for most of his life, it was a pretty neat novelty to set myself into the seat of a big machine. I was enjoying myself, for sure!

The tractor pulled a grain cart that could hold a semi-trailer full of corn kernels. This was big farming right here. My job was to pull alongside the huge combine that was sucking up stocks of corn like Warren Buffett sucking up stocks on Wall Street. It then magically stripped the corn off the husks and spat out kernels.

"Blake, you copy?" coughed the radio on the dash.

Blake reached over and picked up the handset, depressed the transmit button and replied, "Loud and clear Luke. Listen, I'm not the one in the driver's seat today. You can talk to Gary, who's driving the rig. He's new to this, so tell him what you need. I'm in the tractor too in case I'm needed. Over."

"Copy that. Good to meet you Gary. What I need from you is to pull up alongside me. I'm doing 4.4 miles per hour, so dial that into your computer. Once you get to the GPS line on the computer screen, push the remote button. The computer will take over and steer your tractor to follow the line. Over."

After a moment of thinking that Dad never did anything like this, I accepted the transmitter from Blake, pushed the transmit button and replied, "Copy that Luke. I sure hope I can work out the buttons, but I've got a good coach here. Over."

Blake pointed out the buttons to push and explained how they affected the motion of the tractor. Soon, we were following a predetermined line alongside a huge combine that shot bright yellow corns kernels into the cart. Luke adjusted the speed of the combine, quicker then slower then quicker, to fill the cart evenly. I was watching a master at work. All I had to do after plugging in the data was to sit back and watch the little TV screen of the combine firing corn into the cart. The tractor drove itself.

"It's like watching him load gold into the cart!" I said to Blake.

"Naw, it's not like gold at all. Not at less than four bucks a bushel it isn't. It's a really bad year. Closer to coal than gold, I'm afraid."

That put a bit of a damper on my enthusiasm, but only a little damper. I was still having the time of my life.

When the combine hopper was empty, Blake showed me how to take over from the GPS system.

I pulled away from the combine to give Luke time to fill the combine's hopper up again. Once full, I returned to the GPS line so he could continue filling the cart. We repeated the process until my cart was finally full, at which time I took the loaded cart to a waiting semi-trailer.

That's when my stress test really began.

"Okay Gary," Blake said, all business, "the job here is to move the corn out of the cart and into the semi-trailer. The corn will drop out of the bottom of the cart into an auger that will then transfer it up into the semi. You'll need to move the tractor back and forth so that it will load the semi evenly. You want to load it as full as you can, but not overload it or spill anything. Once you're empty, you need to get back to the combine for more corn as quickly as possible. You don't want to leave the driver waiting for any longer than you have to. Time is money."

"Uh, okay," I replied, licking some sweat from my upper lip.

This was not as easily done as said. It was only with my concentration on full that I was able to manipulate the vehicle and controls well enough to do as I was told. This year, I passed the test. I only spilled a half-bushel total, which was not actually all that bad.

"Not bad for an old farm boy learning new tricks," said Blake, wiping his blonde hair off his wet forehead. I guess I wasn't the only one sweating it.

I nodded sagely, as though I'd been doing this all my life, "It's okay, the pheasant and deer love a little corn on the ground."

To my surprise and delight, Blake asked me if I'd like to help out again tomorrow.

"Of course! When you go to Disneyland you don't go for just one day!" I replied with a grin. We agreed to meet the next morning before sunrise at the local Swan's cafe for breakfast.

I woke in darkness before my alarm rang. I turned it off so it wouldn't wake Ginny, pulled on my clothes in the dark, performed my morning ablutions, and quietly slipped out of the house. Blake's truck was already in front of the diner when I got there. We ordered coffee and breakfast as the sky turned from black to deep blue.

"It's quite the operation you have," I said to Blake. "I didn't realize there was so much modern technology involved."

"Well yeah," said Blake. "I couldn't be very competitive if I didn't have all that. Every little bit makes a difference and a farmer needs every advantage he can get."

"I suppose there's just as much risk in it as there was in my dad's day?" I added, "Back in his day, he'd have been breaking his back milking sixteen cows by hand, caring for horses, and running the farm without electricity, praying for the right weather."

Blake nodded and gazed into the depths of his coffee cup. "We still pray for good weather, but there are more modern conveniences for sure. That said," he looked up from his cup to see that I was paying attention, "the risks are huge."

I nodded solemnly to show I was not only listening but respected what he was saying.

"The amount of land we can farm now is enormous compared to what the old-timers farmed, but so is the overhead. We're supporting our families, sure, but we're also supporting an army of workers too. We do what we can. We still have to judge when the best time is to plant, to reap. We're still at the mercy of too much rain, not enough rain, heavy storms, early snow, or God-forbid *hail*. This has been a bad year."

"There's been a lot of rain this summer," I said.

Blake nodded, "A lot of rain and early snow. The moisture content of corn was too wet this year. It never came below 20%, so we had to use the propane driers to get it down to 15%. Higher than 15% and it's too wet to store. All that costs money, and at four bucks a bushel, we're doing a whole lot of work for not a whole lot of money."

"I'm sorry to hear it," I said. "There's a lot of risk in farming. That much hasn't changed."

"Some years you win, some years you lose," Blake said, washing down the last of his breakfast with the dregs of what was in his coffee cup. You just take the good with the bad and hope for more good than bad."

"My mom always said, 'Quitting is not an option.'"

"Your mom was right about that."

As I followed Blake's pickup truck out of the diner's parking lot, I got to thinking about how we're all tested in various ways throughout life. A farmer's life is precarious and full of risk. I thought about Blake and his serious nature. I thought about my parents, always working so hard. Well, I thought, if life is a test, then surely these farmers have passed.

* * * *

4 • BERKLEY WEED WHIP AUTO FEED INVENTION

I GRADUATED FROM HIGH SCHOOL in 1960, and then went to a vocational school in Staples, Minnesota, for a year. I majored in tool design. After that I took a job working with Toro but was only there for a year before moving on to work with IBM in Rochester, Minnesota. I stayed there for a few years but when I took an educational leave of absence, I decided not to return.

I'd noticed that IBM engineers tended to get stuck doing very redundant work, and they also tended to die about 16 months after retirement. I didn't want that to be my future, so I moved on. I went to Rochester Junior College while working at IBM. Then on to the Institute of Technology for three years at the University of Minnesota in Minneapolis.

While at IBM, Ginny and I got married and started our family.

Once out of college, I went to work for Rochester Datronics. There, we designed a mark-sensing computer for automating the marking of school exams. It was good work but when 3M bought out the company, they laid everyone off. They only wanted the product, not the people.

In 1971 I found work at Berkley & Co. in Spirit Lake, Iowa. Engineers were a dime a dozen that year after the lunar landing and subsequent layoffs. They had over 500 applicants for the opening. I think I got the job because I liked to fish!

Berkley Bedell was the owner of the company. He was a great guy; a Democratic congressman who served for 12 years. He was an avid hunter, played tennis, and loved to fish. I worked for him as the chief engineer for seven years designing fishing rods and reels. I got to fish all over the United States, testing our products. It was my dream job!

In the 1970s Berkley had a reputation for making the best fishing line in the industry. So, it was natural that the Weed Eater people from Texas would seek us out to develop a tough line to cut grass and weeds.

We had our own polymerizer to convert monomers into polymers, i.e. fishing line. However, we needed a supply of nylon with which to make the line. In 1974 the OPEC oil embargo was on, so nylon was in short supply. Since we were "just" a sporting goods manufacturer, we weren't high on the food chain for supplies. To address this problem, we bought a depolymerizer from Israel, then bought up used nylon carpeting scraps from Georgia carpet mills. The depolymerizer broke down the carpet into monomers, then we were able to re-polymerize the monomers into fishing line. We were back in business.

We had the ability to modify nylon line to be more abrasion resistant, or to be more flexible. This allowed us to tailor our line to various fishing conditions. I was out testing some stiff abrasion-resistant line for the Weed Eater one day when I discovered a missing design piece for the Weed Whip.

Every time the line would break off at the spinner head, I would have to lay the device down and remove the spinner head and re-thread the line through a guide hole, then replace the spinner head. This was very time consuming and tedious. Even more importantly, if you forgot to unplug the power, one could end up with bloody fingers if the switch hit the ground.

Humm . . . I think there is a better way.

Why not develop a device that would release the line incrementally from the spool?

It has been said that necessity is the mother of all inventions, and so it was in this case. I went to my engineering logbook and made some sketches. I had a design meeting with the model shop, and they built a proof-of-concept model. We tested it by mounting it in the quill of a Bridgeport vertical milling machine. We used a broom to simulate grass. We could trigger what became known as a ground bump device to activate alternating set of cogs to release a new segment of line.

Wahoo! It worked!

We applied for a patent, but unfortunately, we were a junior filing party by two weeks. However, we were granted an interference hearing. At the hearing we were given the patent due to our diligence in reduction to practice. The other party only had an idea and never reduced it to practice. Since then, the patent laws have changed so that now the first to file wins.

Berkley sold the patent to Toro, who licensed nearly everyone in the market space to use it. The royalties were huge. The invention was used on nearly all Weed Whips in the world.

Sadly, even though my name is on the patent, I received no compensation for it. When I went to work for Berkley, any inventions that I developed were assigned and owned by them. I was paid to design and invent so I never looked back. Still, it would have been nice to have received a thank you note!

LESSON LEARNED: Be a business owner not a worker bee!

* * * *

5 • TRANSITIONS

IN 1979, I LEFT BERKLEY and went to work for Hutchinson Technology (HTI) in Hutchinson, Minnesota. There, we worked on printer components and magnetic data storage systems, particularly suspension systems that used chemical etching and lasers.

This was initially a job-shop (a small-scale contract manufacturer) of anything chemically etched, but later we moved into suspension assemblies that held the read-write slider over the hard disk. HTI then morphed into a proprietary product company. The company grew from 100 employees to 3,000 in the nearly 11 years I worked there.

Job shops and contract manufacturers—those companies who manufacture products according to their customers' specifications—traditionally do not make as good a profit as product companies—those companies who manufacture their own products.

With HTI, I witnessed firsthand the transition from contract manufacturing to a product company when we went from building disc drive suspensions to our customers' specifications to building our own proprietary disc drive suspensions.

The transition comes when the job shop becomes so proficient at making the product that the shop knows more about the product than the original equipment manufacturer, or in essence, its customer.

As a job shop evolves, it often develops processes in order to build the product that customers need. Those processes belong to the job shop, not the customer, and the customer generally doesn't have access to them.

We developed and perfected processes that we held as company trade secrets; however, we did not patent them. You might get your patent, but a patent on a process is notoriously difficult to enforce. By patenting a process, you are telling the world what your secret is, and it is easy for your competition to tweak the process and circumvent your patent.

Our job-shop built disc drive suspension units for a few customers. Each customer had its own specifications, so we were building a number of variations of them, but they were all very close to the IBM design. However, we'd developed some processes that could be used on all of them.

We first developed a stamping process to coin the dimple on the gimballing point that was extremely smooth. This allowed the spring to apply pressure to the slider evenly. The second process was to develop a spring that was more stable than our competition's springs were. This involved heat-treating the spring to make it stable and keep it applying the correct pressure to the slider over time, which in turn resulted in a consistent flying height between the slider and the rotating disk.

In other words, we made the disc suspension smoother and more stable than anything on the market at the time.

I was sitting at my engineering desk one day, completely buried in various customers' prints and specifications. They were essentially copies of the IBM Whitney and Winchester suspensions. Each one was very similar to the next and I had to pay attention to the details to keep track of it all. I was so immersed in the materials that I was dreaming about them.

Jeff Green, President of HTI, stopped by my desk and asked, "How are things going?"

I looked up from the depths of paper piles and replied with exactly what I'd been thinking about, "If we tool all these slightly different suspensions, we won't have room for the dies and photo tools in our tool room."

It was true, too. Things were getting crowded, and it seemed to me that there might be a better way of doing things. I asked him, "Why don't we ask IBM if we can use their intellectual property, develop the suspension types, and send it out to all the companies that want a hard drive suspension?"

Jeff scuffed the floor with a shoe. "Think they'd go for that?"

That was a likely response since they were one of our largest customers and what I was proposing would put us in direct competition with them.

I shrugged and said, "Why don't you ask?"

The expression on Jeff's face went from chewing on the impossible to imagining the possibilities. The profit possibilities. His eyes shone like diamond cufflinks. "Well now, I might just do that, Gary."

It would be a tricky conversation for Jeff. If your proprietary process can be applied across different products, you have the making of a proprietary product line. That was the position we were in, but therein lay the dilemma. Would we end up competing with our own customer?

If Jeff asked how IBM felt about our company producing disc drive suspension units based on their design, and they said yes, they would be okay with that, then we would be selling their design back to them as well as to all of their competition.

It would take away their edge, assuming their design was superior to the other designs. They already had a good thing going. Why mess with it? Why allow our company to compete with them when they could stop us before we even had a chance to begin?

Sometime later Jeff stopped off at my desk again. Again, I was buried in paper.

"Hey Gary," he said in a voice that was calculated to sound casual.

"Hey Jeff, how is it going?"

"Pretty good, not bad." He stood there trying to be cool, but I could tell that he was about to explode if he didn't spill it.

"So, I talked to IBM," he said.

"Oh yeah?"

"Yeah. I asked them what they thought about us using their suspension intellectual property, producing them here, and then selling them to everyone."

"Uh huh. What'd they say?" Like I couldn't tell from the huge smile he was trying to suppress.

"Well, they seemed to be okay with it."

"No kidding!"

"Yeah! I felt pretty skeptical about the whole thing, but I figured nothing ventured nothing gained, right?"

He was practically tap dancing. It was contagious and he had me grinning from ear to ear too.

I said, "There were a lot of reasons why they wouldn't have wanted us to do that, why do you think they said yes?"

Jeff nodded, "I had to think about that too. They probably figured that if HTI builds the suspensions for all the competition, that they would get better volume pricing. That will allow them to continue to dominate the marketplace."

I nodded, "Smart like a fox?"

"Pretty smart, that's for sure. It's a win-win for both of us," said Jeff.

Honest communication with your key customer is sometimes the most helpful thing you can do for your own business.

With that one conversation, HTI shifted from being a contract manufacturer to a product company. While we did apply some minor tweaks to the IBM specifications, we still operated within the parameters of their patent.

Our secret processes helped us build some of the best suspension units in the industry. Now, we controlled the product start to finish. This allowed us to have economies of scale such that we had one product instead of several products that were very similar.

We had 80% market share almost overnight.

LESSON LEARNED: It is very beneficial to be open and transparent with your customers, and it never hurts to ask!

• • • •

6 • BIG BIRD OR BIG MISTAKE?

AT HTI WE NAMED MAJOR projects after Sesame Street characters. The Big Bird project was building disk drives for IBM Rochester. We were good at building suspension assemblies, so the next logical assembly level was to make the entire disk drive mechanical assembly. This was to be built in Hutchinson and then transported to Rochester to be merged with the disk drive platters and eventually become a 5 1/4-inch disk drive.

It was an extremely complex assembly where we had to add many new processes. We had to build flexible circuits and populate them with surface-mount technology. We had to inspect the air-bearing surface of the slider. It took six weeks of training an inspector to inspect an air-bearing surface. We also had to stack the suspension arms onto an actuator arm.

We had an extremely aggressive learning curve and production schedule. We put 500 people to work on this project and we went from zero to 1,600 disk drives per day in a seven-month period.

We worked extremely long hours with customer engineers at our site nearly all the time. I remember working late one night, when one of the IBM engineers simply turned his chair towards a corner in the conference room and went to sleep. The next morning, as the sun was coming up, I decided to go home and get a few winks. When I walked into the parking lot, I completely forgot where I'd parked my car!

25

We poured over every last process to look for cost savings. We took out every last penny we could without compromising quality.

The first year of the project was the best. We put about $1,000,000 on the bottom line. The second year about half that and the third year our margins were worse than a grocery store.

That's when Jeff called up IBM and said, "We want out, back up the trucks and take out the tooling."

They sent it to Mexico but never could meet the quality standards that we had achieved.

LESSON LEARNED: Never assume a large company will win in the marketplace.

LESSON LEARNED: It's just as important to know when to get out of a project as to know when to get in.

● ● ● ●

7 • IN SEARCH OF THE TOP QUARK

IN THE LATE '80S, WHILE working at HTI, a very unusual side-track occurred when I collaborated in a project with the Consortium of European Research Nations (CERN) in Geneva, Switzerland.

CERN is a multi-national center for research in nuclear and particle physics. Its main function is to provide the particle accelerators and other infrastructure needed for high-energy physics research—as a result, numerous experiments have been constructed at CERN through international collaborations.

Fun fact: CERN is the birthplace of the World Wide Web.

There in Geneva, they had a particle accelerator called the Large Electron–Positron Collider (LEP), one of the largest particle accelerators ever constructed. In fact, to date, the LEP was the most powerful accelerator of leptons ever built.

For our project, we were attempting to build high purity detector cells for an experiment designed to detect the "top quark." Quarks are the smallest particles ever come across in scientific endeavor. The discovery of quarks meant that protons and neutrons weren't fundamental anymore. Sometimes also referred to as the "truth quark," the top quark is the most massive of all observed elementary particles.

It was the quest to find particles even more elementary than electrons, protons, and neutrons that led to the building of particle accelerators.

The LEP at CERN was a huge round track with a circumference of 27 kilometers (16.777 miles) and was built in a tunnel roughly 100 meters (328 feet) underground. It was situated below the mountains of Switzerland and France. It was used from 1989 until 2000. Around 2001 it was dismantled to make way for the Large Hadron Collider, which re-used the LEP tunnel.

The high purity detector cells we were trying to build were approximately ten inches by 30 inches and three-eighths of an inch thick. They contained up to three layers of detector panels that were connected to feedthrough connections. All of this had to be hermetically sealed and tested with a helium leak detector. Our detector cell was situated at one of the intersection sites—where the particles collide at speeds close to the speed of light.

Working with very high-energy PhD physicists was a very interesting experience and a very different world from what I was used to.

The physicists worked on a campus that consisted of several buildings and a working vineyard. The vineyard produce was not spared at the dining tables. There were several bottles on each table at lunchtime.

Overall the physicists at CERN were very pleasant and we enjoyed working with them. They love to eat and to drink wine. We enjoyed many great meals at many great restaurants up in the French Alps mountains at places I can't even remember and that I sure could never find again. But I sure do remember the fine cuisine.

On one of my many trips to CERN I had a meeting in a building I had not been to before. The entry of the building had a bunch of tags that looked like ID tags.

"What are those for?" I asked a tall man in a security uniform.

In loose English, he replied, "Dey are to detect radiation levels."

"Should I wear a one?" I fingered a tag.

"Oh no, dey don't vork," came the reply. I dropped the tag and felt my stress level move up a notch.

On my next trip to Switzerland, I found out that they did indeed work. Apparently, someone had failed to block an experiment and the whole building was being irradiated! Too much wine? I don't know, but maybe it explained why the physicists had this certain glow about them.

The high purity detector cells were very difficult to make. CERN had originally given the project to a company in France, but that company had failed with the project. I was then invited to France to view the equipment to see if there was anything we could salvage from it.

The laser equipment was extremely complex to the point that it was unworkable. They were trying to weld both sides of the detector cell box simultaneously by splitting the laser beam.

"What do you think, Gary?" asked the French.

I looked at the mess of technology and kind of shook my head and said, "No thanks!"

While I chose not to work with the French to revive their complex laser-splitting plan, I continued to work on the project with the technicians at CERN.

The thin outside panels of the detector cells had to be extremely flat. After shipping several panels, we discovered that they arrived wrinkled in Switzerland. After several discussions with Swissair we concluded that it was the air pressure differential in the airplane's cargo hold that was causing our problem. We then devised a special shipping container to solve the wrinkling problem.

This led to a high-level meeting with Carlo Rubbia, the Director General of CERN at the time. The Director General is chosen for a term of five years from one of the fourteen countries that belong to CERN. Rubbia is an Italian particle physicist and inventor who had recently shared the Nobel Prize in Physics in 1984 with Simon van der Meer for work leading to the discovery of the massive, short-lived subatomic W and Z particles at CERN. When those were discovered, it was felt that the discovery of the top quark was imminent. The detector-cell project to discover the top quark was Rubbia's idea.

The discovery of the W boson further validated the electroweak theory. It also helped to secure the decision to build CERN's next big accelerator, the LEP, whose job was to mass-produce W and Z bosons for further studies.

Because of our shipping problem the project had fallen behind schedule. Rubbia was in a foul mood the day we met with him. With the scheduling problems and his chronic back pain, he was quite miserable. I remember getting off an all-night flight and going into a meeting with Carlo and his staff. I could not wait for that meeting to get over. Everyone in the room took a beating from him that day. There was nothing we could say to make him happy.

LESSON LEARNED: Never go into an important meeting after getting off an all-night flight.

The top quark was eventually found at Fermilab in Illinois near Chicago.

As the SPS gained competition from the Tevatron at Fermilab there was still no sign of the missing particle. After a race between CERN and Fermilab to discover the top quark, the accelerator at CERN reached its limits without creating a single top.

The quest for smaller particles will never end. Hopefully, someday the particle physicists will find the binding energy of matter so that we can heat a whole city with a chunk of coal or some other suitable material.

I am humbled to have been a small part of an experiment at CERN.

● ● ● ●

8 • TRANSITIONS, OR NOT

I WAS A PROJECT MANAGER on a "steel-wheel" project for Hutchinson Technology. We all thought that this would be a great opportunity to make the transition from being a contract manufacturer to a product company. The idea was to replace a molded plastic daisy print wheel that was used for the IBM typewriters or word processors and make a lifetime stainless steel print wheel that would last the life of the printer. The product required many of the existing processes that we were using at the time.

We were successful in developing the product and we did all the necessary marketing research including focus groups consisting of daisy wheel printer users. Everything looked like a go. We went ahead and spent a year developing it—only to discover that customers were perfectly willing to throw away a $30 plastic wheel rather than buy a new lifetime wheel for $150. We had to kill the project.

Steve Jobs never trusted market research. He viewed it as history. We should have had the same view on this project.

LESSON LEARNED: Never trust market research.

Something to keep in mind when thinking about transitioning from the contract work business model to producing your own product, is to keep the two things separate.

Both business models may be perfectly viable but trying to

do them both at the same time, with the same resources, leads to mixed priorities. When the product area is strong with business, the contract manufacturing business suffers from a lack of resources. The customer doesn't know what the number one priority of the company is. It's like trying to serve two masters. Customers need to know they are your first priority, or they will take their business to someone else.

To avoid this calamity the company should set up separate business units without shared resources.

A WORD OF ADVICE: Keep your focus.

Much later, after I went into business for myself with Spectralytics (more on this to come), we had a patented process to make medical stents.

Like earlier with HTI, our process was our own, but the stent designs belonged to the individual customers. Spectralytics tried to make a transition from contract manufacturing to a proprietary product company by designing our own stent. Unfortunately, the cost to develop a proprietary stent was prohibitively expensive. This is notoriously common in the medical products arena.

At that time, it would cost about $50,000,000 to develop and bring to market one coronary stent design. Clinical trials to get to FDA approval were the largest cost. Then, even if we got the hard-won FDA approval, we would still have to develop a distribution channel. So, we remained content to make stents for our original equipment manufacturer (OEM) customers, and a handful of startup stent wannabe companies.

An interesting sidetrack to our contract manufacturing business came when we found out that a stent OEM was using our patented process to manufacture their patented stents.

Johnson & Johnson was the first major producer of the

stent. They owned rights to the Palmaz-Schatz stent. They hired Norman Noble to produce it.

One day, I decided that I would try to secure the business of making stents for Johnson & Johnson, so I hired a sales rep that was calling on them.

"What do you think the chances are that we get this business?" I asked him.

"Pretty good, actually," he replied. "I think there's good reason to be optimistic about it. You've got a good patented process and they have a good patented product. Seems like a good match."

"It could be tough getting the business away from Norman Noble," I said.

"Sure, but I think you have a better manufacturing process. Their process doesn't allow them to put any kind of intricate designs into the stent, but yours does," he said.

"Yes, that's our ace-in-the-hole. It's definitely a better process," I said.

The rep assured me he'd do his best, and I felt quite positive about the whole thing.

Not long later, I was attending a Medical Design & Manufacturing tradeshow in Anaheim, California, where I heard a rumor that my sales rep was selling our patented stent-making processes to Norman Noble. Say what?

I wasted zero time in tracking down the rep, "Who are you working for?" I demanded.

"You," he said. "You hired me!"

"Who *else* are you working for?"

"What do you mean?" he asked cagily.

"Do you work for Norman Noble?" I asked directly.

Red crawled up his neck and into his cheeks and ears. "Yes," he confessed.

I was furious. It was all I could do to contain it. In a low growl I said, "Then I guess you're not working for me," and I fired him on the spot.

Next up, Johnson & Johnson. We started sending inquiry letters to them asking if they were violating our process patent. We got no replies. In fact, we got no replies for two whole years of sending shots across their bow. Finally, we figured if they couldn't say they weren't violating the patent, then maybe they were. We filed suit in 8th federal District Court in St Paul, Minnesota.

That got their attention.

Soon after, we got involved in some court ordered settlement negotiations, however, they were unwilling to provide any reasonable monetary settlement, so we proceeded to a court trial.

The court judge ordered a pretrial negotiated-settlement hearing. On our side we had about three lawyers. On the defendant side there was a sizable battery of lawyers, mostly from New York.

One of the most amusing incidents occurred near the end of the pretrial hearing when our lawyer, Alan Carlson, from the firm of Carlson, Caspers, Vandenburgh & Lindquist, gave a dissertation on how the J&J/Norman Noble legal team should imagine a jury pool made up of an electorate consisting of people who voted for politicians Hubert Humphrey, Jesse Ventura, and Al Franken: respectively, a bureaucrat, a pro-wrestler, and the author of a book titled, *Rush Limbaugh Is a Big Fat Idiot*.

I noticed a somber look from the Madison Avenue defense attorneys. One or two of them even went a little pale.

Alan added, "If this is what you want, well let's have at it."

We had at it. The trial lasted for three weeks of one of the coldest Januarys on record in St. Paul.

We had a great jury consultant from Texas who selected a good jury from a pool of about thirty men and women. I'm not sure it was as convoluted a jury as Alan had threatened, but our lawyers seemed happy with it.

I was the key witness and first on the stand, which lasted about three days. It was the most intense three days of my life. The New York team took every pot-shot at me they could. They challenged my honesty, my reputation, and my very integrity. It's difficult to take insults to my integrity because it's one of the things I take very, very seriously.

After three cold weeks of witness and expert testimony, the jury was sent for deliberation. It did not take them long to reach a verdict.

"We find in favor of the plaintiff." The judge ordered them to pay us $22.3 million dollars.

So, while we never did move from being a contract manufacturer to being a product company, we still did alright. Not a bad sidetrack at all.

LESSON LEARNED: The little guy can win!

● ● ● ●

9 • PARTING WAYS

THINGS WERE GOING WELL FOR me at Hutchinson Technology (HTI), but I was about to learn a couple of painful lessons. HTI was founded in 1965. It specializes in the design and manufacture of precision technologies and had been successfully progressing through the natural stages of the business lifecycle. In the 1980s, the company enjoyed a huge surge in growth, both in terms of revenue as well as sheer size: we'd gone from about 500 employees to 3,000.

I had been experiencing great success as a project-engineering manager of the disk drive product line, and under my management, we had experienced a 100% increase in annual sales about three times. I had been working at HTI for nearly eleven years and fully intended to make it the last stop in my career.

In 1990, because I had been doing such a good job on disk drive components, top management asked me to look for the next $100 million annual sales opportunity. Since I love innovation and new challenges, I jumped at the chance and was eager to move ahead.

Little did I know, or could I anticipate, the perils of such an endeavor.

Management had given me a huge career opportunity, but then they laid down a number of marketing screens. I was to find some kind of opportunity for the company to make $100 million in sales annually, BUT:

- They did not want to do an acquisition; they wanted only a product, not another company.

- The product had to be a component-level product, not an original equipment manufacturer product.

- The product had to be compatible with the existing infrastructure: chemical etching, metal stamping, or laser technology.

- The product had to have high profit margins (a business is said to have a high profit margin when its margin is higher than industry-average profit margins) along with the aforementioned $100 million-dollar annual revenue potential.

I searched the world over and found only one $5 million-dollar opportunity, which was for high-energy physics detector cells at the Consortium of European Research Nations (CERN) in Geneva, Switzerland.

"Not good enough," they told me.

"You're spoiled by the disk drive business. It's unique," I replied. "How often is it that a contract manufacturing company can add an assembly operation to an etched part and end up with a $300 million product line?" I asked redundantly. "Never," I answered for them. "The marketing screens you've given me are unrealistic unless we do an acquisition."

LESSON LEARNED: Never take a job that is highly immeasurable and that has high visibility.

It wasn't good enough.

Top management was not happy with my product-search performance, so they asked me to take a job fixing the flexible circuits product line, which was hemorrhaging badly from bad yields.

Were they trying to punish me? What choice did I have? I couldn't go back to disc drive suspension units, that ship had sailed. So, I went down on the production floor to evaluate the process.

The process was ill conceived at the get-go. It was a batch process and should have been conceived as a reel-to-reel process. Then, I discovered that they were inspecting the circuits *forty-four times* in the process. They were trying to inspect quality in.

When I reported back, I said, "The line is not really salvageable. The basic design itself is flawed. Trying to fix it now would be like putting lipstick on a pig. Plus, with the amount of inspections you're doing, you're wearing the parts out before your ship 'em."

The two top dogs didn't want to hear that either.

"Look," I said to the president, "I can do what I can, but I can't see you giving me the authority or the resources that are going to be needed to fix this product line."

"You're probably right about that," he said.

"Okay, so why don't you give me some other position in the company that I *can* be successful at?"

The two looked at each other for a beat and then turned back to me. Then the one said, "We can get you a six-month severance package."

"Write out a check." I parted with the company.

I learned several things from this experience, including the recognition of the unique set of challenges each stage of the business lifecycle presents for company leaders. One of these challenges is dealing with a mismatch between company positions and the skill sets of the employees in those positions. This mismatch may require a turnover in company personnel. In other words, employees must be repositioned or fired.

Although initially it was traumatic, I realized that it was up to me to decide if this was going to be a traumatic event or a positive event. It was ultimately my choice.

After the initial shock of leaving and not having a steady income, I think losing one's job can make for a better person. However, this only happens if a person rises to the occasion and embraces change and growth and makes the effort to progress on his or her own path.

Personally, I think everyone should be fired at least once in his or her career. We learn through failure. Whether it's being fired in business or failing in some other area of life, we learn from failing and then trying again. It's like what Samuel Beckett said, ""Ever tried. Ever failed. No matter. Try again. Fail again. Fail better."

Once I decided that my termination did not constitute a trauma, I got back up, dusted myself off, and put up my consulting shingle. Believe it or not, I ended up doing some consulting for HTI, whom I ended up staying on good terms with. I worked with other companies as well, but in my heart of hearts what I really wanted to do was to start my own manufacturing company.

Soon after leaving HTI in 1990, I founded Spectralytics. It was the best decision I could have made.

LESSON LEARNED: Sometimes it is best to let go of what you think you really want and open yourself to new opportunities and new paths in your life.

● ● ● ●

10 • COURAGE TO LAUNCH A DREAM

I WAS FORTY-EIGHT YEARS OLD. I was good at inventing things for the companies I had worked for. I'd literally made them millions and then got de-hired. At this point I figured, maybe it's my turn to make some Benjamins!

In 1990, the timing seemed right to start a laser-based contract manufacturing company.

The first stage of any new dream or project is surrounded with wild enthusiasm. I was more excited than a new rooster at a chicken ranch. In the summer of 1990, I rounded up some minority investors and a partner, whom I bought out very early on. We got a bank line of credit and a lot of personal savings and personal guarantees to make it work. We worked long hours putting two laser systems together that would become the tools of our new venture.

The excitement and fears of creating this new company were only interrupted by pizza deliveries. Our first purchase order was for laser-welding jet-engine pressure-sensors in a vacuum vessel. I will never forget driving down I–494 on July 25, 1990, to Honeywell's Solid State Electronics Center division to deliver the first laser-welded hermetically-sealed absolute pressure sensors. It was truly a memorable and exhilarating experience. Then came the next step in most new businesses.

Disillusionment.

At one point I felt poorer than Job's turkey. I sweated things like:

- "Will I be able to keep meeting payroll?" (It seemed like payroll happened every couple of days.)

- "Where will I get the next order from and when?"

- "Will we ever be able to get to break even much less get a paycheck?"

The fear of complete failure. Minor stuff like that.

To start a company, you need several things besides a lot of courage. You need things like a trusting and willing spouse—hopefully one that doesn't know the meaning of personal guarantees!

You need a good marketing plan and a very good salesperson to carry it out. Fortunately, I had Bill who was very instrumental in bringing in sales the first four years.

You need three times more money than you think you'll need.

Finally, you need a good banker, which is rare to find. A good banker might even be an oxymoron.

Fortunately, I had all of these except the banker. Bankers are a strange lot. If you need money you can't have any, if you don't need money you can have all you want!

The lessons I learned in the startup phase were plenty, but as a business owner, the lessons never stop. Here is just some of what I learned along the way.

- Sell the boat; you will not have time to use it. For sure, you will need the money.

- Entrepreneurship is a bad disease and there is no cure for it.

- Quality is number one.

- Laugh at mistakes but learn from them too.

- Nothing happens until a sale is made.

- Never start a company as an equal partnership. There needs to be one strong person in charge, but if you do enter as a partnership, for sure have buy-sell agreements in place.

- Be willing to go two years without a paycheck.

- Listen to your gut. Your master's degree will not help you.

- Pray hard!

Thirty years later I have no regrets. I have made many friends and have many travel experiences.

At one point I felt that I trusted people and employees too much, but in retrospect this was not a regret, because the amount of money I lost by trusting too much pales in comparison to the gains that were made. I have been able to help a lot of people through employment and charity.

It's been a good ride I say! I saw my dreams come true. Sure, I could have done a lot more but in the end it's all dust anyway. Sooner or later someone will trash your trophies. Nobody gives a whit about how big a walleye you caught, or how many points your prized deer had, or how many employees were on your payroll. What people remember is how you treated them, how many laughs they had with you (or at you), and how you touched their lives.

I thank God and all the people that helped me along the way.

And I'd like to thank my son Troy. I was blessed to have him to be a part of Spectralytics the first 11 years. He is an excellent programmer and process engineer. He is a perfectionist and took our stent making process to a new level and was the first employee to work in the Dassel facility. His personality type is close to mine, which presented some challenges. At one point he quit and I didn't hear from for a while, so I had to replace his position. He called me one day and said he bought a boat and rented a house on a canal near Sarasota, Florida, and was fishing every day. I guess that fun got old after a few months. He decided to sell the boat and move back to Minnesota. He wanted to come back to work, but I had already hired an engineering manager. Not wanting to butt heads again, I sold him a laser and had him do our laser marking business, which had good potential. This worked out well. He was also available for some consulting work. In 2018 he moved his business, Laser Dynamics, to Hutchinson, Minnesota.

I'd like to also thank Mark Goemer, a childhood friend of Troy's who was a sales manager and most recently sales director, who brought us to the next level of sales revenue.

LESSON LEARNED: Be nice to the neighborhood kids, they might become your best sales people.

Now, onto the next dream. Remember there is no cure!

• • • •

11 • BEGINNINGS

ONE OF OUR FIRST JOBS was laser welding absolute pressure sensors for the Honeywell SSEC division (Solid State Electronics Center). This was a part that needed to be welded while inside of a vacuum vessel. The sensor would be one of 11 in every single General Electric jet engine. They had to have an absolute zero vacuum reference, which was why they needed to be built in an absolute zero vacuum vessel. The laser beam was beamed through a glass window into the vacuum vessel. The vessel was pumped down into 10-8 torr-liters per second. Then, the two halves of the sensor were put together and rotated under the laser beam and sealed shut by the laser weld. When the completed sensor was taken out of the vessel, it had the required absolute zero vacuum reference.

I was pretty proud of that work. It was an impressive job to take on right out of the gate. In fact, it was so early in our upstart that we didn't even have a name for our company. It was one of the engineers at Honeywell who was instrumental in helping us choose the name "Spectralytics."

Terry came up with the name by using "Spectra" from the light spectrum, and "lytics" which means solutions in chemistry. So that is how Terry came up with the name Spectralytics, and the use of thirteen letters for good luck, and also a name that was a mouthful.

LESSON LEARNED: Customers can be more than just a source of income.

We took a lot on in those first days. There was the job for Honeywell SSEC, and then there was the acquisition. Experts say you should never do acquisitions in your first year of business, but what do they know anyway? We early on violated that principle by acquiring a Wisconsin company called MT Laser. Through that acquisition, we picked up a couple of really good technicians named Al and Ron, a slow flow 150-watt coherent laser, and some low-end CO_2 cutting customers. One of those customers was Cindy Jacobs from Kearney, Nebraska. We laser-cut a ton of wooden plaques for her company.

Another unusual customer we had was the Amish people in Pennsylvania. They sold a number of little wooden toy buggies and we laser-cut out the wagon wheels for them. The irony is not lost on me. Every so often I would get a call from an Amish guy who was talking from a telephone pole in the middle of their compound. It was a bit odd and made for an interesting mental picture as I spoke to him about specs and production.

To make the little wheels, we developed a clever process where we stained some 1/8th inch balsa wood panels. We laid the panels in a vacuum cutter-box with fiber honeycomb inside to support the panels and parts. We'd laser-cut the wheels out of the panel, they'd fall out when we removed the panel, then we took a shop vacuum and vacuumed the little wagon wheels into a bag.

The process worked well apart from an occasional fire in the vacuum box. This created a big panic to shut the laser off and put out the fire. I never really saw it as big danger, but it was very messy to clean up and took a long time to reset the operation. We eventually replaced the fiber honeycomb with aluminum to prevent fires. The aluminum was more expensive but saved the fire mess.

This same process worked for another opportunity that came up that involved cutting sheepskins for 3M. We got a call one day from an engineer at 3M asking if we could cut sheepskins with a laser. Yes, I eventually got used to odd requests. He wanted to cut out buffing pads that were used for polishing new paint on cars. They were unable to find a synthetic material that was as good as sheepskin.

I said, "Why don't you try water-jet cutting?"

He said, "We tried that but it's too messy."

"Bring me a sheepskin. We have a process we developed for cutting balsa wood in a vacuum cutter-box and it might work on sheepskin," I told him.

"I'll be right over," he said.

We put the sheepskin on the vacuum box with the hide up. Then, we adjusted the laser system so it would just barely cut through the leather part. We were then able to pluck the round pads out with very little damage to the fibers—although it did make the shop smell like burnt mutton. This was a great breakthrough and we were able to cut these pads for several years for 3M.

We eventually lost the job to a lower bidder, which turned out to be a good thing because cutting sheepskins was not compatible with the medical products that were starting to fill up our shop.

LESSON LEARNED: Keep an open mind and roll with whatever comes along.

I got a call one day from Michael Oh, a Korean businessman in Manhattan, New York.

He asked me, "Do you know how to cut gold?"

"Yes," I replied, "How thick is your product?"

"It's thin. It's about .01 of an inch thick. It's a cover for a tooth. I want you to cut designs in them and then people can put the gold cover over their tooth."

Like I said, I was used to getting odd requests, so this one never fazed me. "Can you send me a sample?"

"No, I want to come and see you," he replied. "I want to meet you personally because if you become my vendor, I will be sending you about $10,000 worth of gold every week."

"OK," I said. This sounded like it had the potential to be a good contract. "I can pick you up at the airport in Minneapolis."

"Where is Minneapolis?"

"In Minnesota."

"Where is Minnesota?"

"It's in the middle of the country at the head of the Mississippi River."

"Oh," he replied. Then, "Where from Manhattan?" Like he was going to hop in a cab and come on over.

I said, "No, you have to get in an airplane and fly about two hours to Minneapolis. I will pick you up at the airport.

"Oh! Okay! I'll do that. I'll have my secretary book a flight for tomorrow and send you the itinerary."

"Excellent," I said. Later that day I received his flight details.

The next day, I picked Michael up at the airport and took him to our shop in Bloomington. He was sufficiently impressed to leave some samples with me to process. The product line consisted of thirty-four different designs that were to be laser cut into gold metal. The finished products would be used for people to slip over their teeth. The design we cut out revealed the white enamel of the tooth. The designs were anything from a cannabis leaf to the Mercedes propeller logo. There was about a half dozen different sizes to deal with. We machined forms that would accommodate these different sizes. We slipped the tooth form over these mandrels and then cut the design using Michael's CAD file with a pulsed YAG laser beam.

I also crafted a vacuum system to capture the gold dust and gold cutouts. The dust and metal fragments were packaged into a Ziploc bag and sent back with the samples. Michael was very impressed with the results—and with my honesty to return the gold dust and fragments. His previous vendor had kept the scrap and sold it on the side to scrap-metal dealers.

LESSON LEARNED: Give the customer more than he expects.

● ● ● ●

Our first CO_2 laser.

12 • GALWAY BAY

I WAS ON A BUSINESS trip for Spectralytics, traveling from Minneapolis to Galway, Ireland, to visit a few medical device original equipment manufacturers. I was sleepless on the overnight flight from Minneapolis to London and had a six-hour layover in Heathrow airport before my flight to Shannon, Ireland. I had not yet discovered my Tylenol PM trick to help me sleep, in fact, I don't think Johnson & Johnson had even discovered it yet.

I caught a few winks at Heathrow, but I was really tired by the time I boarded the flight to Shannon. My eyeballs were in bad need of a lube job. They looked like two cherries rolled in buttermilk. I squeezed into a seat that was clearly designed to be used only by malnourished elves. I was smashed up against two ladies who must've been on a Christmas shopping trip to London. They had enough shopping bags to stop a truck—or lorry as they're called over there.

I had not reserved a car to get from Shannon to Galway because there were only stick shifts available. Driving on the right side of the road and shifting with my left hand, at night, exhausted, in Ireland for the first time, seemed like a really bad idea. No thanks. I'll wing it. Flying over to Shannon, I looked out the plane window into the blackness and prayed, "God just make it easy on me."

I was prepared to spend an outrageous sum for a two-hour

cab ride to Galway, but surely, I could get a shuttle or some kind of a bus service. When I finally got through customs, I practically staggered into the arrivals area. There, I saw a chauffeur driver with a sign that said "Lone Wolinski."

Now, I know it's a big wide world and everything but really, what are the chances of there being two people on the planet with the name "Lone Wolinski"? I'd wager on none. Zero. Zip. And if there really was only one "Lone Wolinski" I just happened to know the man. He was my engineering contact for my stent customer in Israel! We'd worked together many times.

Knowing that I must have looked like a rumpled drunk in my exhausted state of travel, I nonetheless approached the chauffeur.

"Er, hello there," I began.

The driver, to his credit, did not even bat an eye at my disheveled appearance. In a delightful Irish lilt he asked, "Hello Sir. Might you be Mr. Wolinski?"

"No," I replied. "I'm not Mr. Wolinski, however, we are business acquaintances. I'm wondering if you would mind if I waited with you so that I can say hello to him?"

"Of course not," he replied, and the two of us stood in companionable silence until a familiar tall, dark-haired man approached.

"Lone!" I exclaimed as I extended my hand.

At first his expression was blank. My face was completely out of context there in an airport in Ireland, but after a swift search through his mental Rolodex, recognition swept over him. "Gary Oberg!" he exclaimed. "My goodness! What on earth are you doing here?"

"I'm here on business, Lone. I just got here a few minutes before you and saw your name on this fellow's card. Didn't think there would be two of you with that name, so I thought I'd stop to say hello. How are you?"

We chatted for a brief time and then he asked, "Where are you headed?"

"Galway," I replied.

"Galway! Me too! What a coincidence!" Then, to my eternal relief, he asked, "Do you need a ride?"

"Wow! Do I ever! Thank you."

The chauffeur led us to the waiting limousine. As I eased back into the leather seat, I felt my spirits lift and my energy rally. The long journey was coming to an end as the clock swung past midnight. We spent the next two hours engaged in stimulating conversation that put me in just the right mindset for my many meetings still to come that day. They dropped me right at my hotel doorstep.

We could call this the luck of the Irish, but I am of Swedish heritage. Besides, I really don't think the Irish are all that lucky. They're stuck on a rainy, barren island with a lot of rocks and loads of sheep that smell really baa-aa-aad! I prefer to think of that event as Divine Intervention, but whatever it was, it was more than I could ask for or imagine. I was reminded of the scripture verse in Ephesians that goes, "Now to Him who is able to do exceedingly abundantly above all that we ask or think, according to the power that works in us." I slept really well that night, knowing I was in good hands.

That evening, after my business appointments, I took a walk down to the weir on the River Corrib. It was a nice spring day. The green grass was blanketed with bodies seeking some badly needed rays. Maybe "being lucky" is just another form of "divine intervention." Regardless, looking at the lush green land, the deep blue sky, and thinking about how the last two hours of my grueling trip had prepared me for all my meetings, I couldn't help but think how lucky both I and the Irish were on that day.

* * * *

13 • HOW NOT TO FIRE AN EMPLOYEE IN CHINA

SPECTRALYTICS HAD AN OFFICE IN Tianjin, China. The purpose for the office was to have a full-time sales presence on the mainland. We had an agreement to manufacture coronary stents with Preco Miwa, a Chinese-owned manufacturing company. Unfortunately, my sales manager, Mike, was not securing enough sales to justify his existence. We had a three-year employment agreement and that time period was up, along with Mike's job. I travelled to Tianjin to terminate the position.

I've had to fire people before. One of the worst ones was in Minnesota when I dismissed an employee for incompetence. As the employee walked out the door, unaccompanied, he proceeded to open the gas valves on my most precious gas cylinders and keyed my most expensive lenses. It cost me about $5,000. You'd think that I'd have learned the lesson to not trust a terminated employee, but I'll admit to being a slow learner.

Though I had the proper documentation to terminate Mike, and even though he was an at-will employee of Spectralytics Inc., USA, I soon discovered the challenges of terminating someone in China.

I had a sit-down morning meeting with Mike at the office to discuss the termination.

"Mike," I started, "I think you know why I'm here. As you know, you haven't made a sale in a long time, and Spectralytics can't justify the expense of keeping you on. We are letting you go."

"Letting me go? You mean you are firing me?"

"Yes, we're terminating your position entirely."

Mike looked at me with wide eyes for a long time, then, surprisingly, said, "No."

It was my turn to blink. "What do you mean, 'No'?"

"You don't have the authority to fire me," he said.

"I can assure you, I do," I said.

"No."

"Look," I said, reaching into my case for more papers. I shuffled through them until I found the one I was looking for, "this document shows that I'm the president of the company. If anyone has the authority to terminate anyone or any position, it's me."

He glanced contemptuously at the paper, "You can't fire me in China."

"You're wrong, Mike. I can, and I am, and you are. You need to clear out your office. Now." I was getting a bit miffed by then.

"No, you can't fire me in China," he insisted.

"Okay. Tell me why you think I can't terminate someone in my own company just because we happen to be in China?"

Mike suddenly stood up and walked to face a window that overlooked a lot of other office towers. He shrugged his shoulders and said, "Just can't."

"That's a child's answer Mike." I'd had about enough. "If you can find some evidence as to why I can't fire you, then bring it to me here tomorrow morning at eight. Otherwise, bring a box for your things and we'll discuss the final details of your departure." I stood up.

Mike turned from the window, "I'll see you at eight."

I nodded and walked out.

That afternoon I got a call from the bank stating that Mike had withdrawn approximately $15,000 in cash from our China account.

I immediately went downtown Tianjin to the bank to close the account. Little did I know what that entailed. What had happened was Mike had intimidated Grace, the accountant, to give him her chop. A chop is a seal that is needed on each check. There are two of them required per transaction. Mike had one and Grace had one. By having both chops Mike was able to withdraw the maximum amount per day from the Spectralytics account.

In order to close the account, I had to go to the police department and have published a notice on two successive days in the Tianjin newspaper. This allowed Mike to continue his withdrawal of funds from our account. I immediately contacted the newspaper to publish a notice that our account was closed. In addition, I had to have two new chops made.

By the time this was all done, we lost about $75,000. This turned out to be an expensive lesson in Chinese banking.

Even more importantly, it turned out to be a lesson in not trusting a person that has been terminated.

LESSON LEARNED: No matter how nice a terminated employee seems, walk them to the door. Trust me when I tell you, trust is not an option.

• • • •

14 • ONE ENTREPRENEUR'S CULTURE AND PHILOSOPHY (OR, LUCKY FIRST DATES)

ONE MOONLESS SUMMER EVENING, MY wife, Ginny, and I were coming home from a short boating vacation on the Apostle Islands on Lake Superior. We were in the car, trailering the boat back. As we were heading west from Mora, Minnesota, on Hwy 23, on a two-lane blacktop highway, the headlights blinked out and suddenly everything was pitch black. My eyes couldn't quickly adjust to the blackness and at one point I wasn't sure I was even on the road. I slowed down and drove to the side until I could find a pullout. Fortunately, no cars were following behind me. I pulled into a field driveway and parked the car and boat.

"Oh dear," said Ginny. "I suppose we'll just have to sleep in the cuddy of the boat until morning."

"Why do that?" I asked. "I have a flashlight; the batteries are fresh, and the light bulbs are good. I can fix the headlights right now."

I reached down and felt the car's light switch. "Yup, the light switch is shot. It's hotter than Billy hell!"

I needed a piece of wire, so I climbed into the boat and found a wire that was just the right size and wasn't being used. Returning to the car, I quickly found the wiring harness for the headlights, created a bare spot with my knife and wrapped the wire around it. I then took the other end and fastened it to the positive pole on the battery.

Voila, I had lights.

"Gary! You're a genius!" cried Ginny.

As much as I would have liked to be credited with genius, I couldn't in good conscience. "Naw, I'm just a simple problem solver—a pragmatist. I looked at what I had and what I didn't have. I didn't have a good light switch. All I needed was a by-pass. Problem solved. I like to use the KISS principle."

"I'll give you a kiss alright!" Ginny smiled and kissed my cheek.

I laughed and squeezed her and said, "Not that I'll turn down a kiss, but I meant K-I-S-S, as in Keep It Simple Stupid. It's something I practice every day at work."

We both got back into the car. I turned the ignition key and got us back up on the blacktop. Once we were up to highway speed I continued, "The KISS principle means that I try to keep any unnecessary complexity out of the equation. Whether I'm designing something or managing employees, I find it best to keep things as simple and straightforward as I can."

"That sounds like a good strategy," said Ginny.

I started to warm to the topic and in the dark of the night, with just the beam of the headlights, I felt myself wanting to tell Ginny about my philosophies. She's always been a good listener and I was in the mood to talk.

"When I'm designing a new process, machine, or product, it's important not to involve too many new ideas. One idea that is unproven or untried is enough to deal with. When two or more unproven things are involved your chances of success decrease exponentially.

When I'm designing a new widget or process, I try to get to the hardware stage as soon as possible. This way I can minimize inevitable mistakes before I invest a lot of time and energy into something that has flaws. I'll use bubble gum, bailing wire, or duct tape to prove a concept. Then finish with a good working model or process later. You can learn a lot and gain valuable time from a crude model."

"That makes sense," said Ginny.

I continued, "There's almost always someone or a company that can do something better than you, though. The trick is to find market niches that others don't know about and be the first to capitalize on the idea. Be the lead dog."

"You've done well with that," she said.

"Yeah, I've managed to sniff out a few opportunities."

"How do you manage to use the KISS principle when it comes to people though? People are much more complex than machines or processes," she asked.

I nodded, "You're right about that. I'll tell you, as a founder of Spectralytics, some of my biggest mistakes in business were hiring the wrong people. At one point, I couldn't figure out why my staff at the Dassel facility couldn't get along with each other, so I did myself a favor and hired an industrial psychologist to tell me what was wrong. She administered the Myers-Briggs Personality Type Index to all of our employees. Do you know that test?"

"No," said Ginny.

It breaks personalities into 16 different types based on individual preferences and styles. It's used in business all the time. Anyhow, we discovered that all of my employees were at the corners of the grid. They were all about as different as they could be from one another. It made for some very toxic relationships."

"Where did you fall on the grid?" she asked.

"I'm an INTJ. The "I" stands for introverted, meaning I recharge my energy by being alone instead of being around others. The "N" is for iNtuitive, meaning I focus on ideas and concepts rather than nitpicky facts and details. The "T" is for thinking, meaning I base my decisions on logic and consistency instead of people or special circumstances. The "J" means I like to get things decided instead of leaving them open ended."

"Wow! That's you exactly!" exclaimed Ginny. "Come to think of it, that sounds like a lot of the engineers I know."

I had to laugh, "Yeah, that's what the psychologist said too. She said a lot of engineers are INTJs. Can't really argue with her."

"So, what happened after she assessed all the employees?" she asked.

"Like I said, they were all about as different as different gets and it was causing a lot of grief. What we needed was someone in the middle who could be like a cheerleader, someone who could glue everyone together. I didn't have anyone like that at the time, so I hired Joanne to be my operations' manager. I couldn't have picked a better person."

"What makes her so special?"

"It's a good question. Joanne was a single mom of four, who worked her way through Saint Catherine's University with a double major in social work and business. She worked as a bartender in the evening. She's a really hard worker, so I liked her just for that, but best of all, she had a lot of practice dealing with people and could spot a loser a mile away. Juggling school, work, and four kids was great experience for handling my diverse workforce. To her, multitasking had always been a matter of survival. Now, multitasking is just how she works. It's like she takes all the different people in all the four corners of the personality grid and somehow connects them all. All the friction and personnel grief that we had has just gone away. I have no idea how she does it. Maybe she's the genius."

"She sounds wonderful," said Ginny.

"She is. We're lucky to have her," I replied. "But I still try to use the KISS principle where I can with the people side of the business too."

"How?"

"For one thing, employee benefits. We used to have two categories of absentee. One was vacation time the other was sick time. We used to have employees call up and ask if they had sick days coming before they decided to stay home or come to work. I could care less whether the person was sick or attending his fourth cousin's twice-removed grandson's baseball game. Time off is time off. So, we made a change and simply called it paid time off or PTO."

"That sounds much easier for everyone."

"Yeah. If we have an employee policy that can't be printed on a T shirt, I just don't trust it," I said.

Ginny laughed, "I get that!"

I continued, "Whenever I'm introduced to a new employee, one of the first things I ask them is 'Were you told our company motto?' and if the employee says 'no' I tell them 'Work hard and you won't get fired!'"

"Hah!" she laughed.

I chuckled, "It was always a good ice breaker." Then I added, "I really like to hire intern students for summer work."

"Why is that?"

"A lot of the times, with their fresh eyes they can see things that regular workers can't. They often come up with great ideas. It's a win-win. A lot of the time we'll just give them jobs are not very challenging, but then we'll let them see what other, more challenging and exciting jobs there are too. I'll tell them to go back to school, study hard so they don't have to do this mindless work forever. Also, if they work out well in the summer job, I'll hire them when they get out of school. I'm a firm believer in work-study programs."

"That's great."

"Sometimes, if an employee has made a poor decision or messed up somehow, we'll give them a second chance. Often they turn out to be some of our best and most loyal people."

Ginny was still smiling as she turned in her seat to look at me in the darkness. I could see her outline lit only by light reflected off the highway. "Gary, what kind of boss do you think you are?"

I thought about that for a while as the yellow line droned on and fields ticked past. "Well, I try to practice MBWA."

"Which is?"

"Management by Walking Around."

"Ah. I see."

"Having an open door is a good start, but I find that many people are too intimidated to walk into my office with an idea or a complaint. If I really want to hear from them, I've found that I need to go to them, not the other way around."

"That makes sense."

"Whenever I want to find out firsthand what's happening on the floor, I'll randomly check a part for quality, or I'll check that everyone has the latest specifications."

"M-hm."

"Hah!" I laughed at a memory that popped into my mind. "One day I was out walking the floor, and someone pointed out that I was wearing one brown shoe and one black one. They were completely different styles too! Man, did I take a lot of ribbing over that! I told them I had another pair exactly like this one back home. They laughed but I think it was more *at* me than *with* me, you know?"

Ginny was laughing too and said, "I have no doubt about it! How on earth could you have managed something like that?"

"It was *your* fault!"

"*MY* fault? How do I get the blame for that?" she cried, still laughing.

"I didn't want to wake you up, so I dressed in the dark and must have put on the wrong shoe."

"Oh, my goodness, Gary. Did you tell your employees that?"

"Yeah, but that only made them laugh and ridicule me more."

"I guess some days you just can't win."

"True," I thought about it for a moment and said, "but I think the incident helped me be a bit more human in their eyes. Like if the boss can put on two mismatched shoes because he didn't want to wake his wife up, maybe he's a guy they can come and talk to about an idea or something."

"You're welcome," said Ginny.

"Huh?"

"Well, if it's my fault you put on the mismatched shoes, then it follows that it's my 'fault' that you became more human in the eyes of your employees. So, you're welcome."

I couldn't argue with her logic, "Alright then, thank you!"

"Tell me, Gary. In your opinion—'

"*Humble* opinion," I interrupted.

"Yes of course, your *humble* opinion. What are the most important qualities that an entrepreneur can have? I mean, what makes it all happen?"

"Oh wow . . . That's a big question. I think there are a lot of qualities you need to have."

"Tell me some of them please."

"Okay. Where to start? Hmm . . . I guess first of all, we're independent. I mean, we're not exactly government workers, you know?"

"You're definitely independent, yes," Ginny confirmed.

"You have to be tolerant of failure, because you'll fail. It's a given." I started to warm to the topic. "Entrepreneurs are like mavericks—but not self-proclaimed mavericks. We don't go out of our way to be like that, that's just how we are. We're unorthodox. IQ or degrees don't really matter. We can see opportunity out of problems or disaster."

"Like when you were terminated from HTI and saw it as a chance to start Spectralytics," said Ginny.

"Yeah, like that," I smiled at her. "Let's see, we're driven. There's something in us that just drives us to follow our passion. Without that, we're nowhere. And we push the envelope. We spend a lot of time and resources on research and development. We keep our eye on the prize. We try to keep things in tight compartments and not get distracted from our goals."

"Would you say you're more of a dreamer or a pragmatist?" she asked.

"I'd say I have to be both. To have a successful business, you have to have the vision and then you have to have the problem-solving ability to see it through."

"Kind of like what you did with the headlights tonight," it was a statement, not a question.

I smiled at my wife, once again feeling like I was on a lucky first date, "Yeah, kind of like that, I guess."

"Well, dreamer or pragmatist, I still think you're a genius," she said.

"Whatever I am, I sure am lucky I met you."

• • • •

15 • HANGING AROUND, OR NOT

LOOKING BACK AT THE TIME when we started Spectralytics, and thinking about all the long hours that I would put in, I probably would have gotten out before I got in. If you'd told me then that I'd be working 70-hour workweeks, week after week, month after month, I'd have told you it couldn't be done. However, once you slide into the flow of things, it just becomes your new normal. Thankfully I had a wife who was very understanding and supported me all the way.

So, I stuck it out. I stayed. But that was me. Not everyone decided to hang around.

We had a new hire who was working the second shift. It was his first day on the job and he'd been shown around the place earlier in the day. I know he knew where the bathrooms were because that's where he spent the night.

Spectralytics shared the bathrooms with our neighbors in a flex building in Bloomington, Minnesota, our second location. We had most of the warehouse area but also some office space. Both neighbors had keys to the bathrooms. When the second-shift supervisor closed up for the night, he just locked the bathroom doors like he always did. I'm not sure if he even knew we had a new employee but if he did, he wasn't doing a head count.

The next morning, the day-shift supervisor opened the doors and there was our new guy. He was lying in a corner of the bathroom. He'd pulled out a huge wad of paper towel and made a pillow out of it. Fortunately, he had been wearing a jacket that he was now using as a blanket. When the supervisor opened the door, he woke with a start. The two men stared at each other for several beats, then without a word, the new guy pushed himself up off the cold tile, pulled on the jacket, walked straight past the supervisor, across the main floor, and out the door. No one ever saw him again.

I sometimes thought it probably was a good thing for the company. If a guy can't make it out of a locked bathroom door, he probably wasn't a good employee prospect.

I don't know what it is about some people and their first day on the job, but another time, I was sitting in my office, when for no real reason I turned in my chair and looked out the window. My office in Bloomington had a grand view of the parking lot and the building's front door. I watched as a compact car pulled into a parking spot and a young man climbed out. I didn't recognize him, so I assumed he was the new guy we'd just hired. He looked all right. Nice shoes, nice tie. He looked the building over and began to s-l-o-w-l-y walk to the front door. I saw him square his shoulders, then reach for the handle. The moment he touched it, he jumped back as if it was electrified. He wheeled around and headed back to his car—never to be seen again.

I often wondered what went through the young man's mind as he reached for the door handle. I guess some mysteries are never meant to be solved.

My early partner, Larry, helped with some of the banking and marketing issues in the beginning. As a part of those jobs he needed to speak to a contact in Houston, Texas. He hopped a commuter flight and was in the contact's office by noon.

As he walked into the office the secretary asked him, "What are you doing here?"

"I'm here to see Mr. Jackson."

"Well, isn't that strange," said the secretary, "Mr. Jackson just flew to Litchfield, Minnesota, to see you!"

I guess that's one way to give your frequent flyer miles a boost.

When I moved the company from Bloomington to Dassel, Minnesota, I had to have my space cleared out by a certain date. On that date, I walked around the place, taking one last look.

From the middle of the warehouse floor, I spotted my security camera up in the middle of the ceiling. I had spent about $2,500 to install the system and I wasn't about to let it stay with the building. So, I put a ladder up against the bar joist and climbed up with a wrench to remove the camera.

Of course, as I reached for the bar joist, the ladder slid out from under me, landing with a crash. In an instant I was hanging from the bar joist twenty feet up in the air.

I looked down to the cement floor and decided that dropping down was definitely not an option. I was the last one to leave the building so there was no hope that the crash would summon any help. There was a wall about fifteen feet away with tall shelving up against it, and I realized that it was my only escape route. So, I monkey-barred to the wall and got my feet on the top rung of a storage shelf pin. I was then able to climb down the shelving to the floor.

I dusted myself off and muttered, "Thanks for the save Jesus, but I'm not hanging around here anymore."

I think the camera is still up there.

● ● ● ●

16 • YOU CAN'T BE TOO SAFE

IT WAS A MILD DECEMBER day, the day after Christmas, a holiday for Spectralytics. Only three employees were working that day, Freddie, Lance*, and myself. Freddie and Lance were in the warehouse working. One of the 800-watt CO_2 lasers was not working, so Lance loyally showed up to fix it. I was working off-site for most of the day.

Lance was a guy who would not let anything beat him. He was the best maintenance guy I could have ever hoped for. He was extremely smart and resourceful. He studied the problems to death; he used the internet and any other means at his disposal to figure things out. He had both electrical and mechanical skills, which is a rare talent.

He was also a very safety-conscious guy. This day he was working with a high voltage power supply of 20,000 volts. He was standing on a stepladder with his hand on the power supply cabinet door and in the other hand he was holding a screwdriver. The screwdriver inadvertently touched something it shouldn't have touched.

Kapowee!

Twenty thousand volts shot through his upper body and exited out his thumb to the cabinet door. The jolt sent Lance flying about six feet, slamming him against a nearby storage cabinet. Then, the cabinet rocked and fell, crushing him beneath.

Freddie heard the jolt and crash from the adjacent room and came running to help. Pumped with adrenalin, she pulled the cabinet off Lance but found him unresponsive.

"He looked deader than a fried smelt," she later recounted.

She immediately called 911, and the local Dassel Fire and Rescue Squad was thankfully on the scene in just a few minutes. By then Lance had come around and was coherent. They packed him up and sent him to the Meeker Memorial Hospital.

When I got back to the plant, Freddie filled me in. I immediately drove to the hospital and caught up with him.

"Are you okay, Lance?" I asked, very worried.

"Yeah. I just got zapped," he replied in an "Aw, shucks" kind of tone.

"You darn near electrocuted yourself to death. Freddie told me you were unconscious when she found you. She thought you were dead."

"Well, I guess I was. I don't really remember."

"What do you remember?" I asked.

"I was standing on the stepladder one minute and then I was lying on the floor the next minute." Then he added with immeasurable embarrassment, "I wet my pants, Gary."

"Well, don't worry about that. I won't tell anyone."

"The paramedic told me that's something people do when they die."

"Sounds like you came pretty close to it, buddy."

"I guess I got lucky today," he said.

"Yeah, I guess you did. It seems like you've got more to do before you check out," I said.

Lance nodded agreement, "Seems like." Then he kind of shook off the moment. His face changed and he cheerily said, "Well, I'll be back to work on Monday."

He made it back a month later.

LESSON LEARNED: Always pay attention to safety, especially when around electricity. Keep a hand in your pocket!

*Please note that for privacy purposes, the name of this employee has been changed.

• • • •

17 • THREATS AND CONSEQUENCES

IN 1996, I TOOK A military job for Spectralytics that involved an aluminum fan assembly for the Osprey aircraft. It was an extremely difficult job to do. The tolerances for flatness and circumference were extremely tight. It involved laser cutting and welding and the tolerances that were critical were after welding.

I was late on delivery and I got a call from some Defense Department official.

"Mr. Oberg, please explain to me why you are late with our order," he demanded the moment after I said hello.

"We've been working hard on it but we're having a tough time meeting the tolerances. Just when we think we have it, we do the weld, then the heat from the weld itself causes minute distortion and we're back out of the tolerances. We're trying to figure out a way to work that out and it's taking time."

"Did you not take that into consideration when you accepted the job?" he asked.

"Given the tolerances, we couldn't have foreseen it, so no," I replied.

"Mr. Oberg are you familiar with the Military Procurement Act?" he asked.

This didn't sound good. "No, I'm not."

"The MPA provides the government with the power to seize a business in the event that the business does not make good on a government contract that it has accepted," he said, deadpan.

There was a little hang-time on the line while I took that in. It only took a few milliseconds for me to determine that I would be in trouble if we did not deliver, but what had me scratching my head was the logic of it.

"Are you telling me that if I don't deliver soon that you will seize my business?"

"That is one avenue of action that is open to me, yes," he said.

"How is that going to get you what you want? No one on the planet knows more about this business than we do. Your seizing it will only slow everything down more," I said.

"Mr. Oberg, you are currently in a breach-of-contract situation and this government can and will do everything in its power to see that we get what we've paid for."

I thought about that. It really didn't make sense for them to take over the business and they had to know that. I guess the nature of the Act is to put the fear of God in owners and not necessarily come in and take over. Well, it was working. I had the fear of God in me. I was pretty sure he wasn't bluffing.

"Alright, I'll tell you what. We took the contract in good faith. We believed we could deliver your product within your tolerances and on time. We encountered some unforeseeable difficulties and we're doing everything we can to overcome those challenges. I will personally oversee the project and ensure that it gets our top priority over everything else we have on the go and get it done as quickly as humanly possible," I said.

"That's good to hear," he said. "The sooner the better."

"But I'll also tell you that this will be the last contract I will ever accept from you or the government. You can find someone else to bully and threaten because I don't accept that."

"Well now! You don't need to . . ." and he went on for a while about how I was making a mistake, I was overreacting, yadda yadda yadda. In that moment and even now, so many years later, I knew I had made a sound decision.

I then proceeded to take over all aspects of the process from beginning to end. This meant working two shifts every day until the product was shipped.

I was never so glad to see a shipment go out the door as that one. That was the last military job that I ever bid on or accepted.

LESSON LEARNED: When the ship is in trouble the captain needs to grab the tiller.

● ● ● ●

18 • INTEGRITY

INTEGRITY IS A PRIME INGREDIENT in doing business. Whenever I think of integrity, I think of David Schnur. David founded a manufacturing representative business in California. I love manufacturing representatives. They're basically independent sales representatives. They don't broker or distribute, but they'll help get manufacturers' products to wholesale or retail customers. They provide a great way to get feet on the street without the fixed overhead costs. I have found this to be a terrific way to grow a small business.

When David and I sat down to negotiate his sales commission terms, we agreed that I would pay him a fixed rate for any sales of $500,000+ for one customer in one year. After that first year, the commission percentage would drop for any further sales from that customer.

Little did I realize how big a deal that could be.

We had one customer who did a large amount of business with us and stayed with us for a long time, far longer than one year. However, we continued to pay David the first-year commission fees rather than the agreed-upon lesser percentage. Basically, we fell asleep at the wheel.

When we finally noticed the large commission checks we'd been doling out, we realized that we had over-paid David's company about $100,000.

I called him and explained the situation. "This was our

mistake and I don't want to cause you too much grief. How do you want to handle it? Should we stop paying commissions until the overpayment is used up?"

He quickly replied, "No, I'll mail you a check for the overage."

I was stunned. I had expected to have to work out some long-term agreement so he didn't have to take a $100,000 hit all at once for something that wasn't really his fault. I thought to myself, "This just doesn't happen in this business."

"You sure that's what you want to do?" I wanted to give him an out.

"Absolutely," he replied.

I had a check in the mail two days later.

That folks, is integrity.

• • • •

19 • FUNNIES

I HAVE ALWAYS SAID, "IF you're not having fun or getting enjoyment from work, find a different job." You will never be really successful if you don't enjoy what you're doing. I always tried to find levity in most situations.

I recall a day once when I was walking through the warehouse. I noticed a quarter on the floor. Naturally, I bent to pick it up, only to discover that some joker had glued it down. I heard some snickering behind me and when I stood back up, I found a few of my employees grinning behind their hands. Nodding, smiling, I strolled away—straight to the tool crib. I grabbed a hammer and chisel and returned to the quarter. By now, a fair number of conspirators had gathered to watch the show. *How cheap can he be?* I pried the quarter loose, put it in my pocket, and turned to the perpetrators of this stunt and said, "Who's laughing now?"

The plan was for them to keep lowering the denomination to see how low I would go. Would I stoop for a penny? No one will ever know. Anything for a good laugh.

I've been to New Jersey on business a few times. On one sales call, I met a business owner at his office. After exchanging a brief pleasantry, he started to explain his product idea when he suddenly stopped talking mid-sentence. He squinted his eyes at me, tilted his head, and said, "By da way, I don' have any non-disclosure agreement, but I do have a gun!" as he pointed to his desk.

"Okay, okay!" I stammered. Suddenly my palms were sweating.

"Don' doubt it, Gary. I got it right dare!" He pointed again for emphasis.

"I believe you!" I had no doubt that there was a gun in that drawer.

I left the company thinking, well that was interesting. No business there.

That visit reminded me of an earlier experience with another New Jersey business. We bent over backward trying to satisfy a customer that had a very exacting six-piece laser weldment. When the job was over, I had an even more difficult job of collecting on the job. He'd pay a little. We'd send another invoice. He'd pay a little. We'd send another invoice with a threat. He'd send nothing.

It seems he knew exactly how much to pay the invoice down to. He knew I wasn't going to hire someone to come out there and bust his kneecaps for a thousand dollars. So, eventually I just gave up on collecting.

There are some tough customers in New Jersey, literally.

● ● ● ●

20 • SPIN OFFS

I GUESS A CERTAIN DEGREE of success is measured by how many companies are created by the employees that leave your company and form their own companies. I can name a few.

Whenever a salaried employee came on board, I would have them sign a noncompete agreement. However, most of these agreements aren't worth the paper they are printed on. There is usually a way around them. It never really bothered me though. Rarely did a spinoff hurt my business. I have found that there is enough business in the medical-device contract-manufacturing business for everyone.

I kind of view it as a badge of honor when my departing employees find future success. I always wish them well.

There was a period of time at HTI when we had hired several hundred engineers. Then, we had a few down years when engineers left the company for greener pastures. I always wished them well and was pleased that many became high-level executives in the medical device industry in the Twin Cities Metro area. Some of those people also became successful entrepreneurs in their own companies.

In the end I told myself, "Boy, did we ever do a good job of recruiting engineers!"

• • • •

21 • EXIT STRATEGIES

AS I WAS APPROACHING RETIREMENT age, I started thinking about what the next step was. I wasn't in any panic, but I started to think about my personal future more and more.

One day, I got a call from Tim Burns, the president of a company called Preco. They were a manufacturing company involved in high-speed and high accuracy cutting, perforating, welding, and other specialized industrial processing applications. They were looking for a company that would complement their laser machining acquisition in Wisconsin. I initially told him I wasn't interested.

Not long later, Tim called again. In the time between that first call and his second call, I'd been thinking "'What if." So, when the second call came, I said I would entertain an offer.

I wanted to sell Spectralytics to a company that, first and foremost, would provide a secure future for our employees. I wanted a company that had enough resources to expand the business. What I *didn't* want was a company that was looking for an immediate exit strategy that would flip the company to some large conglomerate.

I also knew that I didn't want to make a public offering, and I would advise any entrepreneur against it. I saw what it did to the management at HTI. It is a big distraction for running a business. It is easy to become defocused from your business model.

After doing our due-diligence work, we found that Preco fit the bill on all counts. I also saw some synergistic opportunities for growth.

They made me an offer I couldn't refuse, and Preco became the new owner of Spectralytics.

The deal met the needs of my minority investors who had been with me as long as a dozen years. I originally wanted to retain 10% ownership in Spectralytics, but that was quickly nixed. However, I did manage to retain a 25% stake in our intellectual property. They also offered me an employment contract for two years, which I was happy to agree to, since that met my personal needs for retirement and continued employment for a couple years.

At the closing meeting, I sat with Tim Burns, the company president, and Jack Pierson, the founder and owner of Preco. We each signed on our respective Xs and that was that.

I turned to Jack and said, "Okay boss, what do you want me to do now?"

Jack looked at me, sort of laughed and said, "We don't operate that way."

I knew that I had found the right suitor.

My original two-year contract to work for them turned out to be a good eight-year run for me, Preco, and everyone. Usually it is a very trying time for an entrepreneur-owner to work for another company that he founded. In my case it worked out pretty well because they let me run the company as I had before. They gave me a lot of professional freedom, which I was grateful for. We had very few disagreements over the eight years.

In 2013, Jack decided he needed an exit strategy for Spectralytics. His initial idea was to get the maximum dollar, irrespective of the goals that I had when I decided to sell Spectralytics. I could see then why he flat-out refused to give me the 10%

ownership when I sold to him; I would have had too much legal power over big decisions such as who to sell the company to next. Still, he probably didn't realize how much I had to say about the final suitor.

I was faced with many interviews with large, billion-dollar conglomerates that mostly had TLA's for names (Three Letter Acronyms). I most definitely did not want to have Spectralytics fall into those hands.

A little aside here. I've heard—the truth of which I cannot vouch—that the word "sabotage" comes from the word "sabot." As the story goes, when French workers in the late 19th century had labor disputes with their employers, they would take off their wooden shoes, called "sabots" and throw them into the machinery.

Now, I was sitting on the deck of Billy's Lighthouse restaurant on Long Lake, Minnesota, one nice summer evening. Across the table from me sat two executives from a large London-based conglomerate. The conversation eventually got around to my role in Spectralytics.

"And what role do you see yourself in, should we purchase Spectralytics, Gary?"

"My role?" I took a sip of my drink, set the sweating glass down on a napkin, leaned in toward them and said, "I can tell you, whatever my role is, there will only ever be room for one asshole in this company, and that'll be me."

With the toss of that wooden shoe, the two executives shifted uncomfortably, picked up their own drinks, and suddenly, "Oh! Look at the time!"

Inexplicably, I never heard from them again. Thank you very much.

Eventually, after vetting many potential suitors, we closed in on an offer from a local Minnesota company. I personally liked the deal because I would get an ownership percentage.

We were sitting in our conference room putting the final touches on it, when a secretary called to say Cretex was on the line. They wanted to make an eleventh-hour offer. Cretex is a family-owned mini conglomerate of medical contract manufacturing companies. I stalled for a couple of minutes for some quick mental gymnastics.

What would this mean for me? For Spectralytics? I probably won't get an ownership percentage. I don't know if they'll want the employees of Spectralytics or just the company. It will probably be a better deal for Jack though, they have deeper pockets.

For Jack, I decided to at least take the call.

I gave the contact information to Tim Burns, and he immediately hit it off with Lynn Schuler, the Cretex CEO. Their deal was an all-cash offer that was considerably higher than what we were working with. While I was correct in my guess that there would be no offer of ownership percentage, it still turned out to be a much better deal for Spectralytics than the offer from the local Minnesota company. Preco was happy. Spectralytics was happy. The deal was consummated very quickly.

Cretex had no exit strategy, which suited me just fine. We were one of six sister companies under that parent company. They did not have a company that had laser technology, so there was lots of potential for cross selling and process synergism. I agreed to a two-year employment contract.

Cretex has been an excellent parent company in many respects. They have invested in facilities, process equipment, and human resources to grow the company for the future. I worked for them for the duration of the two-year contract, and finally, I semi-retired.

I am grateful that Spectralytics is in good hands.

● ● ● ●

22 • TOP 12 LESSONS LEARNED

1. Look for an opportunity in every disappointment. When something bad happens it's rarely as bad as your first assessment. I have found that when God slams a door, he always opens another.

2. Never trust market research. I wasted a lot of time in life designing a product that nobody wanted, despite research saying they did.

3. Be in financial control at all times and remember that cash is king and avoid debt. Be very careful of whom you take investments from and with whom you do business.

4. Stay focused on your business goals. Diversifying can kill you. Behave like a miner; stay on your gold vein until it dries up.

5. Hire the best employees available and spend most of your time with the top performers. The bottom performers tend to suck up all your time with little cost benefit. Hire a few mavericks but not self-proclaimed ones. Some of my worst mistakes were hiring the wrong people.

6. Nothing happens until a sale is made.

7. Give employees professional freedom.

8. When the ship is in trouble you must grab the tiller yourself.

9. Have fun and learn to laugh at yourself. Sooner or later someone will trash your trophies.

10. Be generous with your time and resources. Albert Einstein once said, "Nothing is really yours until you give it away."

11. When you have a product idea, get to the hardware stage as soon as possible, even if it looks ugly, to prove a concept. Then build a final pre-production prototype.

12. Inventory is evil! Nothing good ever happens to it.

● ● ● ●

23 • FINAL THOUGHTS

MY MOM AND DAD LIVED through the Great Depression. This had a lasting impression upon them in the way they conducted their personal life and business dealings. Both sets of my grandparents lost all or some of their farms. This also had to have made a huge impression on my parents.

My dad distrusted banks and even went to the extent of burying cash in fruit jars in our basement dirt floor. After the Great Depression, when times turned better, he elected to save money rather than expand the farming operation. However, no matter how tough things got for my mom and dad, my mom would always say, "Quitting is not an option."

We need to know how wealth is created. Government can't create wealth. Wealth is created when an individual or entity creates goods or services needed by someone or some entity in the world—and that then brings revenue back to the source of the idea. This allows for growth in the economy.

The beneficiaries of that wealth are not only the sellers and buyers, but also the government through tax confiscation. The government can then give back to the people things that we all want like nice roads, schools, and so on.

Despite the fact that my parents were never wealthy, they never once instilled in me class envy. They instilled in me hard work and character ethics. They never envied wealthy people. I am happy for the wealthy; look at all the taxes they pay that we don't have to pay. When I was looking for a job I never once went to a poor person, I received my jobs from wealthy people.

My dad's conservative traits even affected his card playing.

When I grew up, we played Rook instead of regular playing cards. We called it "Baptist Whist" since my mother or grandmother would not allow regular playing cards in our house due to religious convictions.

Rook was a bidding game to see which couple could end up with the most points. The highest bidder could get possession of the kitty, or middle as we called it. It consisted of five cards that you could exchange in your thirteen-card hand, and you also got to name a trump suit color. If you did not make the number of points you bid, you were "set" (put backwards) that amount.

My dad loved to set people, even if he had a good hand to bid. I think that was a result of his difficult life experiences and his consequential conservative behavior. He never wanted to get set, so he seldom got the bidding hand. My playing philosophy was quite different. I always liked to bid and get the middle five cards and be able to name trump. I often ended up winning with my strategy.

I've always liked to swing for the fences.

● ● ● ●

PROFILES

Jeff Green—President of Hutchinson Technology Inc.

Jeff was a Brooklyn Jew by heritage. His dad was a math professor at Brooklyn College. Jeff was a consummate worker and could be seen on the production floor at all times of the day or night. Sometimes you might even find him blowing his tin horn or recorder while walking down the hallway. He loved flying and had a floatplane that he kept by his house. He could land on the snow at the local airport with the floats on! In the spring, he put the floatplane on a flatbed trailer. He would then find a courageous local buddy who would pull the flatbed trailer down the runway above the minimum stall speed with the plane on it. At a certain speed he would rev up the engine and leave the trailer. I thought this was a really nice trick. Some people might have thought it was a bit dangerous, but Jeff knew exactly what needed to happen at the exact time. He was actually very cautious. He wanted an aircraft that had a stall speed that was similar to the continental drift. His aircraft skills paralleled his executive prowess; always on the edge. He could cut through red tape and BS quicker than anybody I know.

John Geiss—Former Hutchinson Technology Inc. Engineer

John was a consummate technologist willing to try almost anything. Including hot air ballooning, growing mushrooms, and rocketeering. He was a chemist and practically blew up his dad's garage when he was a kid. He was a big thinker and wanted to get into the computer systems racket, instead of our seemingly mundane business of content manufacturing. He left HTI on that note and never looked back.

Mike Sokolski—Founder of Rochester Datronics

Mike was half-Russian and half-Polish. He fought with the Polish army in Italy in World War II. He would tell tales of how he traded a gallon of gasoline for a gallon of wine. After the war, he studied in Italy, then emigrated to Sweden where he worked for four years, then he emigrated to the US. He earned a scholarship at the University of Minnesota in mechanical engineering.

I met Mike when I worked for him at IBM for about a year or so. After he left IBM, he started a company called Rochester Datronics. I got a call asking if I'd come and work for him. It wasn't a difficult decision; I was happy to work for Mike. At times he could be very difficult to work with, but we got along pretty well because I knew how to react to his extreme positions.

Mike was a very gregarious outspoken person and an excellent gourmet cook who loved to eat and drink. We connected later with fishing trips to Langara Island in the Queen Charlotte Islands (now called Haida Gwaii) in British Columbia, Canada. I have many fun memories of him fishing salmon and halibut and an occasional lingcod.

Over the years, Mike made 123 trips over 25 years to the Queen Charlotte Islands. He got to know many people from the Haida nation very well and, in fact, because he treated the sea with such integrity, he was made an honorary chief of the Haida nation. This was quite an honor.

As president of Datronics, he sold some stock to some minority investors. That turned out to be a mistake. Through their manipulations, the company ended up getting sold to

3M. Once it was sold, everyone, the whole company, was terminated. 3M only wanted to the product line. It was a blow to Mike.

Mike was a fighter though. After the sale of Datronics, he moved to Santa Ana, California, and became the Vice-President of Engineering for Scantron and did very well for himself.

LESSON LEARNED: Be careful who you sell stock to.

Q & A WITH THE AUTHOR

If you could travel back in time to any country and any era, knowing you'd be completely safe and could come back, where and when would you go?

Skagway, Alaska, during the gold rush days of 1898.

How has your life turned out differently than you imagined it would?

I never thought much into the future. I always thought it would turn out OK and tomorrow would be better than today. It turned out much better than I could ever have imagined.

What have you changed your mind about over the years?

I no longer believe in spanking children. I can now see how bad the liberal progressive agenda is for America. Getting free stuff for able-bodied people does nothing for their self-worth, or a feeling of accomplishment. It creates a victimhood mentality that is very harmful.

Did you consider any other careers? How did you choose?

I originally just wanted to be a draftsman. I always wanted to do something with mechanics and design. I chose mechanical engineering by working as a design draftsman at Toro and IBM Rochester.

How did you end up becoming an entrepreneur?

I have always worked for entrepreneurial companies, except for

IBM. I came of age as an entrepreneur by taking a severance pay at the age of forty-eight and going it alone as a consultant. After a few months of that, I realized I needed some people around me. That was the impetus to found Spectralytics.

Did you always want to be an entrepreneur?

Yes, I never wanted to be tagged to a desk or a specific company. I always wanted to swing for the fences.

What is the best advice you can give to an entrepreneur?

If you are working for someone else, be willing to go to work every day expecting to get fired. Follow your dream.

What mistakes did you make in business and what did you learn from those mistakes?

Testing, testing, testing. It is extremely important to do tons of field testing before launching a product. I find that of most of the products I buy, the designer must never have used it or repaired it.

If you had your life to live over again, being the person, you are today, what would you do differently?

Spend more time with my kids, doing what they want to do, and pushing them to follow their dreams.

What do you think is the meaning of life?

Faith in God, love of family and friends. Leave this earth a better place than how I found it. We are created for a purpose.

What is one of the most beautiful places you have ever been?

Alaska is unparalleled in beauty and diversity in landscape.

Have you ever been a hero to someone?

Brent, one of my employees with a fishing addiction, got in a car accident pulling his boat. During the melee, someone stole the tackle box out of the boat. Brent was devastated. I got the idea to have a tackle box shower for him. I bought the biggest tackle box I could find and had the employees fill the box with tackle when he was off work. His eyes welled up when we presented it to him. He thanked me every time he saw me for a month afterward!

Has anyone been a hero for you?

My dad, he raised three kids on a seventy-acre farm. When he died, he left my mom with a good livelihood.

What is one of your favorite trips that you've taken. What made it great?

A fishing trip to Alaska with my son Troy. Great Silver fishing in a river by Seward and chartering a plane to fly around Mt. Denali on a pristine day and landing on a glacier in fresh snow.

What do you consider some of your greatest achievements in life?

- *Helping Cornerstone Church through a critical time period.*

- *Moving the road away from the lake on Lake Manuell.*

- *Starting Spectralytics and growing it into a stable growing company.*

- *Inventing the auto feed mechanism for the weed whip.*

- *Developing manufacturing processes to make suspension assemblies for HTI.*

What is one of the greatest physical challenges you have ever had to go through?

Field dressing a large bull moose and getting it back to camp by sundown.

What are the top three greatest challenges you faced as an entrepreneur?

- *Financial viability.*

- *Managing a diverse group of employees in Spectralytics in Minneapolis metro in the 90s.*

- *Finding a location and building for Spectralytics growth.*

How far back can you trace your family ancestry?
1800s.

Have you participated in any competitions?
Skiing, fishing, golf.

What makes you happy?
Strapping on my rifle and heading up the mountain to my elk blind.

What is your best advice when it comes to work?
Enjoy your work or you will never be successful at it.

What gives you peace of mind?
The knowledge of working hard and accomplishing a goal.

What books have really made a difference for you?
The Bible; Every Good Endeavor; Good to Great; Surprised by Faith; Against all Odds

Who have been the five most important people in your life?
My wife and children: Ginny, Dawn, and Troy. My good friend Quintin Clark. My dad and mom.

Do you prefer summer or winter?
I love all seasons, but fall is the best: hunting deer, ducks, elk, moose.

What things are you proudest of in your life?
Building Spectralytics into a strong viable company.

What have you overcome in this life?
Fear of public speaking.

Are you a morning person or an evening person?
Morning.

What has made your faith stronger?
Going through tough times with Spectralytics.

Have you pulled any great pranks?
The fishnet prank on Larry. (This is one of the stories featured in my other book "Sidetracks: 40 True Stories of Hunting and Fishing on Paths Less Traveled.")

What simple pleasures of life do you truly enjoy?
Watching the sunrise from a duck blind or hunting spot.

What have been some of your life's greatest surprises?
How fast time goes. I guess it's not that life is so short, it's that we are dead so long!

TIMELINE

1942–1950—Early years of growing up on a farm learning about nature and growing things.

1950s—I attended School District 51 for eight years in Rose City, Minnesota. I was the only boy in a class of six students. I couldn't graduate soon enough. I was bored silly and wanted to go to Alexandria to attend high school. I lived twenty-two miles from school so there was no chance for me to participate in sports after school.

1960s—I attended Staples Area Vocational Technical Institute in Minnesota and received a certificate in tool design in 1961. Then, I went to work for Toro as a draftsman in Minneapolis.

1962—I went to work for IBM in Rochester, Minnesota, and shortly thereafter married Ginny, my present wife of fifty-eight years.

1964—I took an educational leave of absence from IBM and attended the University of Minnesota full-time, majoring in mechanical engineering.

1967—I graduated from the University of Minnesota with a bachelor's degree in mechanical engineering and went to work for Rochester Datronics. We designed and built mark-sensing equipment used in schools and for voting machines.

1971—Rochester Datronics was sold to 3M, which left me having to find a job that summer.

1971—I started working for Berkley, the fishing tackle company, in Spirit Lake, Iowa. I started as a fishing reel designer and then migrated to fishing rods. This is where I designed the Weed Whip auto feed.

1978—I started work at Hutchinson Technology Inc. in Hutchinson, Minnesota.

1979—I was the project engineer who developed the first laser welding system to weld the three-piece Winchester suspensions assemblies for disk drives.

1984—I was the program manager of the Big Bird project for IBM Rochester. We made the major electro-mechanical portion of a 5 ¼" Pixie disk drive.

1989—I left HTI and did consulting work for Checkpoint Systems, an RFID (product security tags) company in Puerto Rico, among other companies.

1990—We incorporated Spectralytics and built two laser systems in the spring and summer months. We shipped the first order of absolute pressure sensors for the Honeywell SSEC division in Plymouth, Minnesota. Our first location was on Bush Lake Road in Edina, Minnesota.

1991—We acquired a CO_2 laser company located in Wisconsin.

1994—We laser-cut the first prototype coronary stent for SCIMED Life Systems and in Maple Grove, Minnesota.

1995—We started a shop in Raleigh, North Carolina, to make heat exchanger plates for APV Baker.

1998—We bought a 21,000 square foot building in Dassel, Minnesota, and started moving portions of the company there.

2005—We sold Spectralytics to Preco, a Kansas company.

2006–2010—We started an infringement lawsuit against Cordis, a division of Johnson & Johnson. A successful trial ended with a $22,350,000-dollar jury award for us.

2013—Spectralytics was sold to Cretex, a mini conglomerate located in Elk River, Minnesota.

2017—Spectralytics opened a 25,000 square foot research and development facility in Maple Plain, Minnesota.

ABOUT THE AUTHOR

GARY OBERG, BME, PE has spent his life on the edge. As an engineer, successful entrepreneur, and Founder of *Spectralytics*, a company providing laser processing solutions for medical devices, he's taken a lot of chances. But he really learned about risk mitigation over a lifetime of pushing the limits outdoors. He grew up on a dairy farm in 1950s Minnesota, where he learned to appreciate nature and her ways, and spent much of his life fishing and hunting throughout North America.

Gary is the author of the bestselling book *Sidetracks: 40 True Stories of Hunting and Fishing on Paths Less Traveled*, a collection of stories from his over 70 years of outdoor adventures and the lessons they taught him. Written as the sequel to his popular *Sidetracks* book, Gary's new book *My Sidetracks as An Entrepreneur: True Stories and Life Lessons for Successful Business Leadership* shares stories from his life in business.

Gary has a mechanical engineering degree from the University of Minnesota and worked for companies such as IBM, Berkley Fishing Tackle Company, and Hutchinson Technology before founding his company Spectralytics Inc. in 1990. In 2012, Spectralytics was purchased by Cretex and became part of the Cretex Medical family, a family of manufacturing companies offering contract manufacturing of medical devices.

Gary and his wife Ginny reside in Litchfield, Minnesota, and Tucson, Arizona, where he continues to enjoy the great outdoors and live life on the edge. As he says, "If you're not living on the edge, you're takin' up too much room."

Gary's books are available on Amazon in both eBook and print. Visit his website at www.mysidetracks.com for more information.

Made in the USA
Monee, IL
12 April 2023